Adventures Within

Confessions of an Inner World Journalist

By

Joe Vitale

ISBN: 1-4107-7459-7 (e-book)
ISBN: 1-4107-7460-0 (Paperback)
ISBN: 1-4107-7458-9 (Dust Jacket)

Library of Congress Control Number: 2003095764

This book is printed on acid free paper.

Printed in the United States of America
Bloomington, IN

Proofreading by Jenny Meadows
Design and Layout by Jill Weimer

1stBooks – rev. 08/04/03

Dedicated to

my parents,

with total love

Table of Contents

The world's greatest hypnotist, boxer, magician, preacher, and writer is born. It all begins here, with abusive childhood experiences, ESP, mind power, magic, and an ancient Chinese symbol that just wouldn't let go…

Bhagwan Shree Rajneesh was the most notorious spiritual teacher this decade ever saw. He was expelled from the USA as a national criminal. Every major country denied him entry. Why was this gentle-looking old man treated this way?

You can change your past and anything else you want. Barry Neil Kaufman, founder of the Option Process, has cured autism, cancer and other "incurable" challenges. he says "You never, ever, have to be unhappy again."

Meir Schneider was born blind. He was declared hopeless and given a certificate of blindness. Yet today Meir not only can see, he drives a car. He has taught thousands world-wide to overcome their physical limitations and has a 95% success rate!

Stuart Wilde is a metaphysical English rogue who plays Mongolian war games of the mind. Learn how you can control your destiny, have astral sex, read minds AND get rich. Find out why this unusual teacher's favorite mantra is "WAM!"

Imagine a sizzling bed of red-hot coals on the ground in front of you. Feel the heat. Now see yourself STEPPING on those coals! Save yourself a blister or two in this chapter.

"est" was THE controversial seminar of the '70s. It's back. Only now it's called "The Forum" and they let you go to the bathroom. What happens behind those closed doors? Why is Erhard's training like "surgery with a rusty knife?"

Which come first, your thoughts or your feelings? Is you unconscious mind in you head, your body, or out in the spiritual world someplace? Meet Milton Ward, founder of Instinctive Yoga, and discover Focusing, too.

Do you create your own reality? Robert Fritz has designed a breakthrough course on how to create the life you want. But is ideas differ from most. For one thing, they work! Learn how to become "...the predominant creative force in your own life."

If you want to face fears, transcend difficulties, get tested every day, confront your ego, and grow beyond belief, go into business! It is the only guru that will never fail you.

WARNING!

What you are about to read may shock you.

Most of it took place more than twenty years ago. I wrote it more than ten years ago. I decided not to publish the material at that time because I found it too personal and too intense. The first two chapters alone are not for the faint of heart.

So why am I publishing it now?

After my book *Spiritual Marketing* became a #1 bestseller at Amazon, I realized just how many people wanted to know my whole story. Many asked me what took place before I met Jonathan, the spiritual healer I wrote about in that book.

I didn't pay very much attention to those requests until my most recent book, *The Greatest Money-Making Secret in History!*, also became an international bestseller at Amazon. That's when even more people wrote to ask me to explain my life journey. Many said they wanted my complete autobiography.

As I mentioned, I wrote most of this material more than ten years ago, back when I was struggling, starving, and unknown. I had little published, I still lived in a dump in Houston, and I was desperately going for, yet merely crawling, to get to my dreams.

I shoved aside the material now in your hands for more than ten years because I wasn't happy with myself. I had experienced decades' worth of bizarre activities, from fire-walking to guru-worship, and I had little to show for it. I wanted results and wasn't seeing any. I was embarrassed to release this book at that time under those conditions. So I put this book on a disk and hid it, even from myself.

I found the disk in June of 2003. Tom Parish managed to decode the files, as I had written the chapters using a software program that wasn't around anymore. And Jenny Meadows read the book, letting me know I should indeed publish it. She said the first two chapters were hard to get through because they were so intense, but the rest of the book was " ... interesting, fascinating, evoking, thought-provoking and informative."

You're about to read the earliest parts of my spiritual journey. I think you'll find it interesting and maybe even inspiring. Keep in mind that it was written well over ten years ago. This was a part of me that has evolved into who I am today.

And keep in mind that what I learned through pain, you can learn through reading.

In other words, where I went through some intense and some odd experiences to achieve the insights I gained from them, you can acquire the same insights from just reading this book.

With that in mind, turn the page . . .

Dr. Joe Vitale
August 2003

INTRODUCTION

June, 1990

Earlier today I zoomed down wet Houston roads to attend a new seminar called "Design Your Life." I fought with myself the whole rainy drive there. I kept thinking I should be home working on my latest book. At one point my car skidded around (on the freeway!) 180 degrees---aiming the car back home. Yet I still didn't get the hint.

One hour into the day-long seminar a woman sitting next to me, my partner in an exercise to clarify values and goals, looked at me and said, "What are you doing here?"

"What?" I asked, surprised.

"You could teach this seminar," she said. "You've done more workshops than the 200 people here. I can tell that from the way you do this exercise. So why are you here?"

I laughed out loud. I realized I had not been true to myself and was delighted to have the real me identified. It took a stranger with a loving heart and an alert mind to tell me what I already knew.

I've done twenty years' worth of work on myself through various seminars, workshops and classes. I've walked on red-hot coals in a sizzling firewalking seminar. I spent two entire weekends in a locked room with Gestapo-like encounter group leaders. I spent seven years with the most notorious guru in the world. I've been in personal-growth situations so intense my nose bled. And I have interviewed gurus, teachers, seminar leaders and "New Age" celebrities.

That woman was right. What in the world WAS I doing in this seminar?

I thanked my wise partner and left the room at the first break. I drove home (without a skid) and resumed work on my latest writing. I did not need to complete the "Design Your Life" seminar to know that *Adventures Within* is the project that has the most value for me right now.

Adventures Within is the true story of my twenty-year adventure through various gurus, seminars and New Age events. The book, in my opinion anyway, is part autobiography, adventure story, self-help book and teaching tale. My intent is for these pages to inform you of what it is like to do unusual seminars (like firewalking) or to be a disciple of a controversial man (like guru Rajneesh). I also want this book to inform you of teachers and methods that are valid (like Meir Schneider healing the blind or Barry Neil Kaufman curing autism). And I want this story to blow the whistle on areas that are often too easily accepted (like channeling) or too easily dismissed (like the power of belief).

Writing this book has been a hoot. A hoot and a holler, actually. I've finally gotten to tell my story. ALL of it. Whenever I've publicly talked about my experiences, I've held myself in check. I was never too explicit, or too honest. Not even with myself.

Here, in this book, I've let it all out. Edgar Allan Poe said that you can't write a totally honest book without burning up the paper you write it on. Well, your fingers ought to be feeling some warmth as you turn these pages! (And if you don't feel the heat, turn to Chapter Six and read about firewalking!)

I've written this story as much for me as I have for you. I want you to understand my life, but I also want to share some thoughts with you that will make a difference in your own life. Most of us live pretty predictable lives. I want this book to expand your boundaries and dissolve your limitations.

I want to help you reach your own inner world.

Enjoy!

Joe Vitale
Austin Texas

www.mrfire.com

Chapter One

THE FORBIDDEN ZONE

The Making Of An Inner World Journalist

You are probably wondering how I got dragged into the counter-culture movement called the "New Age." I've wondered about it myself. Sometimes I think that I had little to do with it. It often seemed like a hand other than my own led me down these odd paths. But shirking responsibility won't explain why I did what I did.

The best I can do is describe some of the events of my life. Then maybe you will understand why I found the "forbidden zone" of life more attractive than everyday reality. I have always been curious about life. It's this trait of curiosity, and my desire to escape the pain of my childhood, that made me search for a new way of being.

BORN EARLY

I was born at an early age. My father was an electrician and I was his first shock.

Actually, my Dad was a railroad foreman, ex-Marine and prizefighter, who was so grateful for the birth of his first son that rainy winter day in 1953 that he went to a church, fell to his knees, and thanked God.

That gratitude quickly slipped away, however. My father treated my mother and me as members of his platoon. He was authoritative, strict, macho and, at times, cruel. I've since learned to understand the pressure he was under, so I'm not writing this to make you feel sorry for me. The facts are simply facts.

My father was from the old Italian school that said the man was the head of the house and had complete control. The stress he was under from believing that myth was awesome. Though Pop worked out every day, running, skipping rope, and punching a bag in the garage, he often lashed out at his family. It was never pleasant. But since I was a child with little power of my own, there was no escape.

I recall the time my father shoved me into a pool of warm piss. I was probably sixteen years old by then. I couldn't stop wetting the bed. It was humiliating beyond belief. And it was uncontrollable. I've since learned that it happened because of my fear of my father. He scared me. His behavior frightened my brothers and me so deeply that we only really let go at night, in sleep, and the results were disastrous.

The urine would eventually burn a hole in my mattress. The hole would gradually enlarge, and sometimes the pee would gather at the bottom of the bed in the plastic of the lining. When the plastic couldn't hold it any longer, the lining would break like a water balloon and the pee would flood the floor. It was an awful, smelly, embarrassing sight.

I recall one day when my father blew his top. Men were bringing in a new mattress for me. My mother, brothers, sister and grandmother were all present. When the delivery men picked up my old mattress, the plastic lining broke and the yellow poison hit the floor. My father lost control. His neck thickened. His eyes were those of a wild animal. He used to talk about having a killer instinct when he was boxing. I saw it in him right then. I was terrified. The back of my neck felt vibrant with fear.

He put his big hand on my neck and shoved me to the ground. He pushed my face in the piss. I couldn't resist him and I didn't dare try.

"Put your face in it!" my father roared. "Get a taste of it!"

I was crying. My mother was terrified but couldn't move. My grandmother, my father's mother, told him in her thick Italian voice to stop. After a few minutes of this torture, my father let me up.

That sort of abuse isn't easily forgotten. Or forgiven. Writing about it now makes my skin crawl. I eventually stopped bed-wetting, of course, but it was not a conscious decision. As I grew, I somehow changed. But I never forgot the years of extreme abuse and humiliation.

ELECTRIC LASH DANCE

I remember walking with my two brothers to a corner drug store one Fall day. I was a teenager, the oldest in the family, and the caretaker of my brothers. My brothers were throwing stones at houses. I told them to stop, but they knew I had no real authority. They kept throwing. And then a woman came running out of her house and rounded up all three of us.

This big, mean woman took us in her house and made me call my Dad.

"You don't want me to do that," I said.

"Call him right now, or I will!" she demanded.

You can imagine what happened. In minutes my father was on her front porch, red-faced, angry, ready to kill.

He grabbed one of my brothers and began to whip him with his belt. My brother was dangling in the air as my father held one of his arms with one of his own and beat my brother senseless.

The woman saw my Dad's fury and rage and yelled for him to stop.

"Take them home and beat them," she said.

I am certain she regretted having me call my Dad once she saw how he handled his kids. But she didn't stop him. "Take them home and do it," she repeated. "Don't do it here!"

Dad threw us into the car, rushed us home, and battered us as we went into the house. We didn't make it past the front door before Dad had us crying and screaming and falling down in pain. His belt felt like electric slashes across my skin.

I covered my head and yelled, "MY HEAD! MY HEAD!"

I acted as if I had hit my head on the door so Dad would stop killing us. He did stop. Just long enough to check my skull. And then he resumed lashing us.

I was beaten the worst. It didn't matter that I never threw a rock at that woman's house. I was "in charge" and should have stopped my brothers. Years later my parents would still say I was guilty of it all. I never forgot what happened---more the unfairness of it all than the whipping.

I don't blame my father. What he did was terrible. Today he'd be locked up for child abuse. But he was acting out of a mindset that said he had to beat his kids to get them to listen. He didn't see any other choice.

Years later, when I was married and struggling through financial hardships, I got a taste of what Dad must have felt. He never beat me on a daily basis for my bed-wetting, only when he had to buy a new

4

mattress. It was that action that hurt him. It reminded him of how little he had, how hard he had to work, and of how many bills he was already dealing with. He didn't need another mattress in the budget.

I related to that feeling when my wife and I needed a new car and had no money. Or when one of our cats bit into an electric cord and required emergency treatment, and we had nothing in the bank to pay the vet. It hurt. It hurt in the same way it must have hurt my Dad.

The difference is that I didn't beat up anyone over it.

SEEKING PEACE

There had to be something better!

The reality I had as a youth wasn't happy. There were happy moments, of course, but all in all, it was the pits. When we were getting ready to move into the house my father built by hand, my mother said, "We'll have everything we need there---and there will be a belt hanging in the basement for Joey's whippings."

My beatings had become an accepted way of life. And I was only a teenager.

A friend once attempted to justify all the beatings I went through.

"Your father taught you to be obedient," he argued. "You learned never to be bad."

"Naw," I countered. "I learned never to get CAUGHT being bad."

"But the spankings taught you to be a good person, didn't they?"

"I was a good person before the whippings," I said. "And I'm one now. Look at my sister. She's raised three children to be honor roll students and they are all popular and healthy. She never hits them. She treats her kids with respect, not like animals."

My friend seemed to understand my point. But I had to add one more comment. (I like getting in the last word.)

"If you treat people with respect, they learn self-respect," I said. "But if you beat them, you teach them they are no good. Their self-image is that of a slave."

Not liking what I had made me want something else. And that's when I began to explore the alternatives. Where some kids may do their escaping and exploring with drugs or alcohol, I chose the region of my own mind.

My curiosity about life was strong, but I learned to move within strict parameters. I was cautious---more like terrified---of doing something that would upset my father. So instead of looking outside myself, I began to look within.

I read books on ESP, psychic phenomena, hypnosis, ghosts, mental telepathy, magic, and much more. Claude Bristol's classic book, *The Magic of Believing*, was my introduction to metaphysics. It taught me about the awesome power of your own mind. Once you could hold an image in your mind with such vividness that you could see it, touch it, taste it, even smell it and hear it, then you would probably bring that image into reality.

Another powerful book---and one I haven't found in two decades---was called *How to Strengthen Your Life With Mental Isometrics*. It was by an English hypnotist named Sidney Petrie and a freelance writer by the name of Robert Stone. I recall that book's making a deep impression on me. It, like Bristol's book, taught me that your mind was more powerful than any man-made tool.

Robert Collier was another influence. His famous mail-order books taught me that positive thinking could lead to positive results. I read *The Secret of the Ages*, his classic, and *Riches Within Your Reach*, another wonderful Collier book. They each painted a picture of a heaven on earth---all created with your mind.

I was a member of the ESP Lab, too. Al Manning and his ghostly friends were getting a lot of my money. Because I had lied about my age and spent the summer of my 16th year working on the railroad, I had lots of money. I didn't have a car, wasn't paying rent, and had no bills. So I spent nearly everything on self-improvement. I took a correspondence course in using the *I Ching*, the Chinese *Book of Changes*. I bought reel-to-reel tapes of Al Manning channeling answers to my questions about life and sex (mostly the latter). I purchased Al's books, tapes, powders and so forth. Al Manning was such a big part of my life at that time that even now, twenty years later, I think of him with a warm smile.

I was 16 and wanted a wise friend. Spirits seemed like a relatively safe bet. I put one of Al Manning's tapes on my machine and relaxed. Al began to channel "Professor Reinhardt," his own spirit guide. As I listened, I became terrified. What if I DID meet a spirit teacher? A ghost? What if it spoke to me? Or---dear God--what if it wanted to TOUCH ME!?

A breeze lightly slid across my face. Was it a spirit? Was it a female spirit? Would it care to make love? Since I was a virgin, that thought didn't help me relax any.

I heard the floor crackle as if someone were walking on it. It didn't take long for me to get up, switch the tape machine off, and dart out of the room. I wanted to meet my spirit teachers, but I was far too afraid to allow it to happen. Still, for several days after the event I had the odd sense that "someone" was watching me....

The mind fascinated me. I knew we could do things beyond belief and I was willing to try anything (except meet invisible dead people).

I recall trying to walk through a wall. I had been reading that everything in life was energy, that your hair is energy, and your body, and the walls, too. So I figured I could walk through a wall if my energy was right. It never worked, of course. I could never get my energy "right" for that feat.

I suppose I wanted to have a super-mind so I could beat my father with my wits. Fighting him on his own turf wouldn't work. He was too trained as a killer. His favorite book was called ***Kill or Be Killed***.

So I used my mind. But I soon learned that he would simply dismiss what I learned. I remember telling him, "Pop, did you know that when your will and your imagination get in a battle, your imagination always wins?"

It's a psychological fact. I had just read about it and was very impressed. Not my Dad, though.

"That's not true," he said.

"Yes, it is. I read it in a book."

"Books aren't always right, Joey."

You can see my predicament. Try to win with my body and he'd easily beat me. Try to use my mind and he'd simply contradict what was said. It was very frustrating.

THE WORLD'S GREATEST MAGICIAN

I read a lot of biographies. Whether it was about Daniel Boone or Harry Houdini, I learned that people usually had a lot of struggles in life. I wasn't alone. And I learned that people usually triumphed, even when the odds looked hopeless. What it took was hope, a dream, guts, perseverance, and luck.

Since my father was too overbearing to allow me much freedom in how I acted, I used my mind to be an adventurer. Reading books gave me safe but exciting experiences. The odd thing is, the books began to nudge me out of my shell. They inspired me to take action. They made me thirst for the life they described.

After reading about Houdini I decided to be the world's greatest magician. Came up with a name and even invented a few card tricks. I used to let my brothers tie me up with rope in the basement so I could practice being an escape artist. I always got out, too. No knot could hold Excello!

And I practiced holding my breath. My plan was to be tied up and thrown over the bridge in my hometown, right into the river. I saw it as a major media event. Even then I was thinking of my image and conjuring up publicity stunts. I don't know why it never occurred. Maybe fear got the best of me. Maybe my father stopped it. I don't remember.

I have never lost my interest in magic, however. One of the reasons I began to explore the metaphysical movement was because I was looking for REAL magic. I used to be very disappointed that the magic tricks I bought and learned were just that: TRICKS!

One day I bought a trick called the "dancing hankie." Supposedly you pulled a handkerchief from your pocket and it danced in front of you, on the floor. I bought the secret to the trick. When I read the instructions I was amazed to find out you had to have wires to make the hankie dance. I had actually thought the hankie would dance as if alive. I remember putting it on the floor and saying "DANCE!" When it didn't move, I read the instructions. It was a profound disappointment.

What I wanted was real magic.

THE WORLD'S GREATEST BOXER

My father had been a boxer. Supposedly he was pretty good, too. I read a lot of bios of fighters and became fascinated. They were colorful characters. I began to worship people like James J. Corbett, the man who beat the famous John L. Sullivan. Few knew that Corbett had written his autobiography. I, of course, read it.

I read about Gene Tunney, the literary fighter who beat Jack Dempsey. One of my all-time favorite boxers was Floyd Patterson. Floyd always seemed to be such a gentleman. I met him when I was a kid and it was like meeting God.

Floyd had just beat some local boy in a Cleveland bout and he was heading to his locker. I climbed all over seats and ran down aisles and jumped a fence to be able to put my hand on his shoulder. Floyd was the biggest, strongest man I had ever seen. I wanted to be like him.

Though my father could have coached me, I did my training on my own. I was serious, too! My training consisted of running several miles a day, punching a heavy bag for hours at a time, skipping rope until the whizzing cord became a blur, doing push-ups, sit-ups and more. Every night I would lie in bed and see myself as the world's heavyweight boxing champion. Everything I had learned from Al Manning, Claude Bristol, Robert Collier and the others came into play. I'd see myself in the ring, triumphant, and see my hand raised so everyone knew I was the winner.

I was in the best shape of my life at this point. And then I walked down the stairs to the basement where my father, sitting in a chair at the base of the steps, said the line that blew it all apart.

"You're in great shape," he said. I looked at him, wondering what was next. "But you'll have to struggle with being overweight all your life."

I was stunned. Crushed. Devastated. Destroyed. I believed that my situation was hopeless. I had worked hard to be in top physical condition. Now I was being told that in my father's eyes I'd always have "a problem" with weight.

At that moment I gave up.

THE WORLD'S GREATEST HYPNOTIST

For a while I wanted to be a hypnotist. I read a dozen books on the subject and found a friend willing to be my guinea pig.

I put him in a trance and told him, "Your hand is numb. You will now feel an ice cube against your hand."

And then I placed a lit match on his skin.

"That's cold!" he said with a smile.

Another time I told him to ask his deeper self what job he should pursue.

"I see a clock," he said. "Every fifteen-minute section is a different job. I guess those are my possibilities."

"What are the four jobs?"

"They keep changing," he said. "I guess I don't know what is right for me."

Though that experiment was a little frustrating, I was impressed that my friend was able to get an answer from his subconscious.

But our experiments weren't always successful.

I had been reading about age regression and wanted to try it out on Bill, my brave friend and subject. I put him in a deep trance and led him backwards in time. When I got him to five years old, I asked him to tell me his age.

"Seventy-two, how old are you!?" he said, laughing like an impish child and slapping both his knees with his hands.

"Now Billy, tell me how old you are."

"Seventy-two, how old are you!?"

This wasn't going anywhere so I decided to wake Bill up. Clapping my hands together was the cue for him to wake up. I said, "Billy, you will awaken now." And I clapped my hands.

Billy laughed uproariously. He sounded like a little kid who wasn't going to listen to his elder.

I slapped my hands together again. He laughed.

Oh hell, I thought.

"How old are you, Bill?"

"Older than you, big nose blue!"

I panicked. How was I going to get him back to his right age? How was I going to explain to his mother that he was no longer 16--- that he had been regressed to the age of five!? With my excellent visualization skills, I could easily see myself in jail for tampering with Bill's mind.

In my research into hypnosis I had learned that there were a couple of clinical hypnotists in Cleveland, Ohio. I decided to call one. I knew this was an emergency. I had to do something. And fast.

"I need to speak to Dr. Carlston," I told the secretary or nurse who answered the phone.

"Regarding what?"

"It's an emergency," I said, trying to sound like an adult with a serious concern. "It's real important."

In a moment I had Dr. Carlston on the line.

"Yes?" he said. He sounded like a cigar-smoking Freudian analyst. His voice was gruff.

"Ah, sir? I have a question for you." I was nervous. Only a few feet away Bill sat in his chair, laughing like an idiot. I wondered if the doctor could hear.

"What is it?"

"My name is Joe Vitale and I am studying hypnosis."

"You're what?"

"I'm studying hypnosis. I was wondering what you should do if, ah, a person doesn't come out of a trance."

"Are you playing with hypnosis?"

"No, sir. My friend and I are just studying it and---"

"You kids better not be fooling with hypnosis!"

"No, no, no!" I said, my voice cracking. Billy was still laughing in the background. "Just, what happens if a person doesn't come out of a trance?"

"I'm too busy to answer these questions," he said. "Call me tonight when I have time."

"Wait!" I yelped. "Dr. Carlston, well, to be honest, I have my friend in a trance and he can't get out."

"YOU WHAT!?" he roared.

"We were doing age regression and--"

"Jesus! You can cause trouble! What's the matter with you kids? You can't play around with something as powerful as hypnosis."

There was heavy breathing on the phone. I knew enough to be silent. Finally the doctor spoke.

"What's your friend doing right now?"

I looked behind me. Bill was sitting in his chair, still cracking up in laughter over some inside joke only he knew about.

"He's laughing," I said. "He's probably about five years old."

"God! Well, he'll come around. The trance will wear off or he'll fall asleep and wake up. He'll be okay."

"He will?" I asked. "Should I do anything?"

"You should stop playing with hypnosis. It is a profession and a skill and not for kids."

"I won't do it any more," I said.

After I hung up the phone I went over to Bill. I clapped my hands and said "Wake up!"

Bill blinked. He looked confused for a moment. He looked up at me and said, "I dreamed I was about five years old."

"I don't wanna do hypnosis any more," I said.

THE WORLD'S GREATEST PREACHER

When you think about your life, all sorts of images rush back into your mind. Some of them you didn't even know you had.

I had entirely forgotten that at one point in my teenage years---the turning-point years for me---I wanted to be a religious leader. I had been brought up in a Catholic family and was very confused about their way of life. My second-generation cousin, a priest, didn't help any. He's a fascinating man. Speaks nine languages, born in Rome, Italy, was once a prisoner of war under Mussolini, was twice put in front of a firing squad and---seconds before his death---was saved by a Catholic-loving German.

For a long time Catholics weren't allowed to eat meat on Fridays. My cousin was in a restaurant with my family one Friday and ordered a hamburger. Everyone looked at each other. Finally my father, the bravest of the group, spoke.

"Excuse me, Father, but isn't today Friday?"

"Yes."

"Well, you just ordered a hamburger."

The waitress brought the hamburger and set it in front of the priest. My cousin looked at the thick meat on the greasy bun and moved his hands over it, saying, "In the name of the Father, Son and Holy Ghost---now it's fish."

It was that sort of ironic behavior that confused me. I thought I was going to be a priest for a while there. I visited a couple of priests in my hometown and asked them about it. They were moved by this teenager's desire to be holy. One touched my cheek and blessed me. I remember going into the church afterwards and praying. When I came out, the world seemed filled with light. I felt as if God had washed the planet. Everything was alive with a glowing energy that made me feel wonderful.

But the inconsistencies of the church and its practitioners didn't sit well with me. Fear was the primary motivator. Either go to church and pray or go to hell later. Some choice. And since I was already afraid of life, going to a place where fear was reinforced and even rewarded didn't seem fun. So I quit.

I visited the Mormons for a while. The story of Joseph Smith discovering a new Bible and seeing spirits intrigued me. A couple of missionaries came to the house for a few days and taught me the principles of Mormonism. I even went on my first fast with them as a cleansing process before I was to be baptized as a Mormon.

But then my Dad stepped in.

The night before my scheduled baptism, Pop confronted the two young Mormon teachers who had become my friends.

"I've been listening to you two for several weeks now," Dad told the Mormons sitting at our kitchen table. "You've brainwashed him to think your way is best. Well, it isn't!"

Though surprised, the Mormons were cool.

"We invited you to sit with us so you could understand what we were telling Joey," one of them said.

"I listened to your talk from the other room," Pop countered. "It's ridiculous. I'll give you an example right now. You said everyone should give ten percent of their income and they'll get richer."

"That's right."

"Come on! You expect the people starving in third-world countries to give away their last money? You expect people in poverty in the hills of the South to give up ten percent of whatever they have?!"

"Yes."

Dad turned to me. "You see what they're saying? They want people to give money to THEM so they can keep going!"

"But Dad---"

"I want you two to get out of my house," Dad told the two guests. "You've brainwashed Joey to think like you. Get out of here. Now!"

Needless to say, they did.

My next stop in my search for a spiritual-religious path that would satisfy me---and maybe my father---was with Billy Graham. I loved his rousing talks. I remember reading about his works and liking his more positive approach to religion. Pop seemed to like Billy, too.

I looked into Evangelism and read books about Billy Sunday, the predecessor of Billy Graham. The "come down here and be saved" speakers, like Sunday and Graham, had a charisma and power that was nearly irresistible. They were practiced orators. They knew how to work a crowd.

But what bothered me about them---and about nearly every religion I visited---was their dismissal of the more metaphysical or inner aspects of life. Psychics and ESP and spirits were generally seen to be the work of some devil. I could not buy that idea. It sounded limiting and self-righteous. I somehow knew that a religion had to contain all of life to be valid. You couldn't say you were right and dismiss everyone else as wrong, as many fundamentalists did. The world was too big. There were too many cultures for one single religion to say they and only they had all the answers.

So my search continued. At times I felt like an agnostic, someone who wanted to believe in God but wasn't so sure He was around. At other times I was an atheist, flatly refusing to believe in any sort of deity.

I recall blaming "God" for many of the woes of my life. One day I was exercising in the basement of my parents' home when I heard them fighting upstairs. My father was bellowing at my Mother, and Mom was barking right back at him. I heard them and felt my body fill with anguish. It was unbearably painful.

"You call this life?" I said out loud, wanting my words to somehow reach "God." I was angry and addressed my pain to God. "If you're around, stop them from fighting!"

I waited. My parents continued their verbal battle. I stood downstairs, tears on my face, and listened.

I concluded God was either not home, not listening, or not existing. None of it made me very happy.

THE WORLD'S GREATEST WRITER

Somewhere during all these experiences I realized that I could be EVERYTHING I wanted to be by being a writer.

Books had become such an important part of my life that I realized writing them could be incredibly rewarding. And I had been reading a lot of material by Rod Serling, the creator of *The Twilight Zone*, and I knew that I could act out any role I wanted---from boxer to magician to preacher to anything else---by simply writing about it and putting myself into the writing.

I put myself through a self-study program that still amazes me. I read every book on writing. I did all the exercises every author suggested. I'd spend hours at the library working on articles, researching, developing my style and learning my craft.

When I was about 17 years old, I got to meet Rod Serling. He was to give a lecture in Youngstown, Ohio, and I made sure I was in the front row. I had always admired Serling's creative talents. I was anxious and excited about meeting him.

It was disappointing, however. He was a little man in an average suit with a silly, up-tight smile on his face. His upper lip was frozen to his upper teeth. I suppose I had expected him to appear on stage in a cloud of smoke and dazzle us with his verbal skills. Again, I was looking for real magic. What I got was life. What a disappointment.

Serling was human. Though he often wrote chilling stories, he said that "If there were a bump in the middle of the night, I'd be the first one outside in my skivvies." He had been a boxer, too, and said, "I was the only fighter to be carried both in and out of the ring."

Serling was open and likable, but certainly not the God I had imagined him to be. He talked about being a writer, and said that he often had his ideas rejected. And he said that making his first sale as a writer was more exciting than making six figures for a screenplay he wrote.

At the end of Serling's talk he invited questions. I raised my hand and asked him, "Do you plan to write an autobiography? Why or why not?"

I was very nervous and the words machine-gunned out of my mouth. Somebody in the row behind me laughed. But Serling seemed to understand the question.

"A biography of myself?" he asked. "No, I don't think I'll ever do that. I really haven't done anything with my life, so I think my autobiography would be pretty boring."

I was grateful to have spoken to Serling. But I think his answer revealed how little he appreciated his own life, his own uniqueness. He never did write his own story. It was a great lost to us, I think, because he died a few years or so after I met him.

But I was now hooked on writing. I loved creating stories and molding words into sentences that made people laugh or cry or think or feel. And being a writer was right in alignment with my budding metaphysical interests. Though I didn't realize it at the time, I had entered a profession that was highly spiritual or "inner-oriented."

Most writers don't know where their writing comes from. James Dickey said his writing surprised him more than it did any of his readers. Minister Eric Butterworth said he sat down at his typewriter every day and just hit the keys. Sooner or later he'd stumble into a rich vein of ideas, and his next book would be on the way.

When I write, the words float up from somewhere inside me and enter my mental awareness. At that point, I write them down. But my writings come from a deep well within me, not from my conscious mind. And that's where there's a link with spirituality. Whenever I go into the "writer's trance"---as horror-meister Stephen King calls it---I experience this otherworldly, ego-less dimension of pure creativity. It has helped me become aware, sensitive, empathic, curious, wise and, I hope, readable.

William Saroyan, to give you one example, was a famous author who deeply influenced me. I even wrote a play about him at one point. There was something about his writings that walked, talked, lived and breathed. I remember an early Saroyan story, probably written in the thirties, where the lead character is in a bus accident. He tells the girl beside him, "It'll be okay. Just be a witness to it all."

Being a "witness," or an observer, is a highly spiritual discipline. It gives you perspective on life. It helps you detach from pain and suffering.

But how did Saroyan, an American-Armenian with no interest in spirituality, know about "the witness"? I've read all his books and all the biographies on him. There aren't any references to Saroyan and the East. Yet he obviously learned a major secret of life somewhere along his journey. My guess is that it came to him as a by-product of being a creative writer.

As I learned about writing and writers, and as I practiced my craft and learned to surrender to the impulses urging me to write, I slowly discovered the healing power of creativity. I teach a popular workshop called "Writing For Transformation," where I help people experience this aspect of writing. Everyone loves it. One woman said, "Your class has been more therapeutic than my seven years of therapy!"

It's not me. Or the class. It's the power of creativity expressed through writing. I'm convinced all writers have touched it---and loved it so much that they took to drink when they weren't creating from it. Real life just doesn't compare.

Despite all the adventures I'll describe for you in this book, despite my discoveries and breakthroughs, at the heart of my journey has been creativity. I am in love with creativity and I believe I am here to inspire creativity in you, and in everyone else I meet. Creativity is simply an inexpensive high which can transform your life. It's a soul drug.

It's been said that "In the beginning was the word." I say, "In the beginning was silence, and what we've done is cover that silence with words." Writing, for me, is a way to unravel our story so that we can return to our essence.

You can use the experiences of your life to create from. Or you can invent from the material at hand. Mark Twain, for example, simply stretched the reality of his life to come up with entertaining material. My wife is often amazed at how quickly I can develop an entire work of fiction as a tangent to something that happened in the day. She teasingly says I have "a quick little lying mind."

"I prefer to call it being creative," I reply.

There aren't any pointless experiences. Child abuse, hypnosis experiments, boxing, magic, and writing are all part of the package called "me." Each has given me unique insights and talents. The experiences of our lives are the herbs and spices that make us delicious. I wouldn't eat garlic by itself (though my brothers once ate an entire string of garlic bulbs to get even with my father). But put a little garlic in my chili and it's a delight!

You, too, are composed of unique spices that make you a savory meal. Take the spices of your life and create with them. You can create a book, a song, a painting, a carving, or anything else that comes to mind. When you do so, you will experience the healing power of creativity.

Here's a quick example for you: When I was in college I lusted after a lass called Wendy. But Wendy never lusted me back. It was a case of unrequited love. What I did was write a play, put her in it, and then kill her off. My drama teacher loved it. It was very therapeutic for me as well.

One more example: Years ago I walked into Dallas with no car, no money, no job, no friends, and little hope. I went to a job interview at a major newspaper. The man interviewing me was very cold and shallow. He reminded me of a computer program. When I got home I wrote a story about a man who goes for a job interview and is interviewed by a robot. My main character got to outsmart the robot in the story and come out on top. That, too, was therapeutic.

You get the picture.

But there's something much more wonderful that comes from visiting the "forbidden zone" of life. When you totally surrender and allow your mind to play, your ego lets go, your editor takes a break, and something deeper arises from within you. It's very empowering.

I know many therapists and educators who are still looking at their pasts and weeping. One friend says, "You have to release the bodily held emotions from the abuse." Another says, "Forgive them and go on."

Every path is valid for some people at some time. The trouble comes when we try to sell it as a universal cure-all. Writing, for me, has helped me make sense of my life. As a journalist for the New Age movement, I have been able to keep my wits about me in order to report on what I was experiencing. But no writer is objective. We view life through our perceptions and speak from our preconceived ideas. I've been caught up in events, too.

Leo Buscaglia, the famous speaker and author on love, says he had a happy childhood. He affectionately talks about his father and mother and their years as a family. But I once read an article which included a quote from Leo's brother. "Who is he talking about?" his brother asked. "Our family life wasn't like that at all."

It's all in how you choose to view it. Though I'm not delighted that I was abused as a child, I accept what occurred. It's what has made me. If it's true that we actually select our parents and our destinies before our birth, as some leaders suggest, then there must be a REASON for it.

But looking for a reason is a very head-oriented exercise. It may be wiser to accept who we are, where we're from, and then choose where we want to go. A wise man once said, "When you wake up, get up." The past needn't be carried around. You can drop it right now.

When I teach writing classes, I often drive to the meeting room full of worries and concerns and plans and agendas. But when I get there, I leave it all at the door. I simply drop the mental luggage and do the class. We can do the same with all of life.

As Jane Roberts' Seth has said, "The point of power is now."

Chapter Two

THE ORANGE BLOSSOM TRAIN RIDE (AND CRASH) OF RAJNEESH

If you're over 40, you've heard of Rajneesh. I guarantee it. For several months in the mid-'80s he was in every newspaper in the country. Bhagwan Shree Rajneesh was the white-bearded Indian guru who led one of the largest---and most controversial---spiritual movements in the world. He is also the man labeled "the sex guru" and "the rich person's guru." Bhagwan became the most notorious religious leader of the decade. He had a hundred Rolls Royces and a half million disciples. After he was deported from the U.S., no country would allow him entry. For a while I wondered where Bhagwan's jet would land.

Rajneesh is dead now. He died in January 1990 at age 58 of apparent heart failure. His disciples say he won't come back because he was enlightened and fulfilled his destiny. Metaphysical people say Bhagwan died because of a lack of love in his life, which ruined his heart. Politicians everywhere are just glad Bhagwan is dead. They never liked him.

I was a disciple of Bhagwan's for more than seven years. And since I never officially turned in my disciple papers, I suppose I might still be considered a "sannyasin" of his. I ran Bhagwan's Houston meditation center, I visited Bhagwan twice in Oregon, I sat before him when he was in silence, I sat before him when he was giving discourses, and I arranged major publicity events for him in Texas.

People wonder why. Why did this good Catholic boy turn to the East for inner fulfillment? Why did this middle-class, Ohio-bred young adult dress in orange clothes and a string of 108 wooden beads? Why did this employee of Exxon wear a locket with Bhagwan's picture in it---even when Bhagwan's face was pilloried on the cover of every major magazine and newspaper? Why did this reasonably intelligent writer maintain his love for his teacher even when the guru's movement was accused of embezzlement, attempted murder, sexual misconduct and political misdeeds?

I'll tell you why.

TAOISM

Throughout my life I've been plagued with a symbol. When I was a teenager I saw this symbol on milk cartons, railroad cars, even books. I was not hallucinating. The symbol was always the trademark or logo of some company. What I couldn't understand was why so many companies used it. Or why it seemed to haunt me so much.

The symbol, I learned when I was about 16, was the ancient Chinese yin-yang symbol. You've seen it. It's a circle split in two by a curved line, one side dark, the other side light-colored. Sometimes there is a dot of white in the dark half and a dot of black in the light half. The image refers to balance in the world. Man and woman, light and dark, goodness and badness. It is generally considered to be a symbol of the Taoist religion.

I didn't learn all of this at once. It took time. First I saw the symbol everywhere I turned and wondered why the hell it stood out to me and no one else, and further, what the hell did it MEAN?

I was a member of the E.S.P. Laboratory out of Los Angeles and I asked the director, Al Manning, what the symbol meant.

"It's a sign from your spirit guides that they are around," he said.

"It is?" I asked. "How come they don't just phone?"

Al didn't laugh. He took his séances and psychic skills pretty seriously.

Years later I learned of the Taoist link. By then, I was married and living in Houston. Still confused, still searching, still tired of struggling thru life as a poor college student or an unhappy truck driver (my job at the time), I went into Houston's most famous metaphysical bookstore.

Aquarian Age is located in a big house in the Rice University area of central Houston. When I first walked into the place I was impressed with all the books lining the walls. They had everything from philosophy to astrology to odd-ball stuff like "pyramid-power" and "gemstone energy."

But what got my attention---I can see it even now---was a line of books on the right side of the store. They were all by the same man. Rajneesh. He had books on Zen, Christ, Buddha, and---you guessed it---Taoism.

I picked up the book on Taoism. On the cover was a photo of the author. I didn't like his looks. He had a black beard and, as I recall, a bare chest. And he was Indian. I couldn't connect with him. But I did note his eyes. They were large, dark, and very bright. Something about his eyes held my attention.

I opened the book. I read a few lines. As a person who loves books, I am always eager to experience a new author and a new style. Rajneesh's style was lyrical, gentle, and wise. The words touched me. I don't at this moment recall what I read, but I know it stuck with me.

It took some discipline to not buy the book. But I managed to leave it at the store. For then.

My job required me to make a long drive to the place where Texas's most famous ice cream is made. All the way there, as I drove that big truck up and down the small hills that grow near Austin, I kept thinking of Rajneesh and his book. By the time I returned to Houston I was sold. And I went and bought the book.

That night my wife and I took turns reading from the pages. We were deeply impressed. Something about this man's words seemed true. It was as if he spoke from a place of knowing that I couldn't even fathom. And he had a way of weaving stories and jokes into his message that was unforgettable. And irresistible.

I read more books after that. A spending spree began that nourished my soul but emptied my bank account. No matter. I was improving myself and feeling happier. Besides, money is material and I wanted the spiritual. At least that's how I thought then.

Taoism was no longer my main concern. Though my wife made a wedding band for me with the yin-yang symbol engraved on it, and though Taoism seemed like the best religion for me, I was onto something bigger. Rajneesh had no limits. He could speak of Zen and Taoism as easily as he could tell jokes or quote psychologists or physicists. He seemed to be a genius. A living orator with the ability to kidnap minds with his words.

I was hooked. As I read, I learned he was a guru. He had disciples, called sannyasins. He had an ashram, called the largest growth center in the world, right there in Poona, India.

You can imagine what happened next. First I toyed with the idea of becoming a disciple. I was never good at decisions. This wasn't any easier. But one night I had a vivid dream where Bhagwan showed up. He and I were sitting in a room. It felt like India, but who could tell? I told this bald guru I was thinking of being his disciple. He smiled that warm, contagious, loving grin but said nothing. I said I wasn't sure. He said three words---I still can't remember the three words---that told me to become a disciple. When I awoke in the morning, I wrote Rajneesh a letter and requested *sannyas*.

SANNYAS

The mailman is my best friend. It doesn't matter if I know him or not. What matters is that he (or she) brings me books, tapes, letters, catalogs, packages, checks, and so forth. Every day is like Christmas---if it's a mail delivery day---because you never know what the postman will bring. He never has to ring twice at my house.

Bhagwan's letter arrived in September of 1979. It was a sunny day. I saw the tan envelope in my mailbox and I skipped back inside. I was elated. Tore open the envelope and there was my new name. Swami Anand Manjushri. A note said Anand meant "bliss" and Manjushri was "a disciple of Buddha." What an honor! My ego soared!

Didn't know how to pronounce my name, though. Went to the library and they shrugged their shoulders.

"Learn Sanskrit," a librarian said.

One day I was leaving a post office when an Indian was walking in. I flipped around and got his attention.

"How do you pronounce this name?" I asked. I showed him my sannyas name.

"Easy. En-nawn Man-jew-shree."

From then on I used my sannyas name. It wasn't easy. One day, while going to a temporary assignment, I introduced myself as "Anand Manjushri" to the red-neck employer. He looked stunned.

"Say what?" he asked.

I repeated my name.

"You from around here?"

"Ohio."

"You got a nickname?"

"You can call me Joe."

Well, I did my best.

My biggest problem was with my landlady. She was in her seventies and a Sunday school teacher. When she noticed my orange clothes and mala---a string of wooden beads and the sign of a Rajneeshee---she got worried.

"Why are you looking to India?" she asked me. "What's wrong with our religions?"

"Well, do you eat only American food?" I said, figuring I had a strong case for an argument brewing. "Other countries offer something different. Maybe even better."

"What does food have to do with it?"

I could see she wasn't understanding. I decided to use the direct approach with her.

"I have looked into what we have here and they are lacking," I said. "They argue with each other, they all use the Bible but still disagree, and none of them have ever made me feel happy."

She let it go, thinking I was a nice guy and sooner or later I'd come around to my senses.

The biggest argument was with my father.

I had sent my parents an article I had written, paying homage to Rajneesh. In the piece I told of my conversion, my happiness, Bhagwan's books and meditations, and much more. My folks didn't like it. Though they were two thousand miles away, I felt their anger.

"What are you doing with this Rajneesh guy?" my father said over the phone. "What happened to you?"

"He's a genius, Dad."

"Joe, that man is a newcomer."

"A what?"

"A newcomer."

"What's that?" I asked.

"He hasn't proven himself. He's too new."

"He's proven himself to me, Dad."

"He won't last," my father said. "You need to get away from him now."

"Dad, what does his being a newcomer have to do with anything. That's senseless, Pop. He's alive so of course he seems like a newcomer to you."

"Then you want to say Marconi was a newcomer!"

"Huh?!"

"You think Columbus was a newcomer too?"

"Dad, what are you talking about? Bhagwan is a wonderful man. Have you ever read his books?"

"No, and I'm not going to!"

"Then how can you say ANYTHING about him?"

"Listen to me, I know about people like him."

"Dad, you don't know anything about Bhagwan. If you did, you'd be happy for me."

There was a short pause on the line.

"He's got you brainwashed, huh, Joe?"

That did it. I broke down. I cried. And I hung up. For the first time in my life, I hung up on my father.

Crying, hurt, enraged, confused by my father's insane arguments, I paced the room. I felt like thunder and lightning were playing tag in my stomach. The rain fell down my cheeks as I sobbed. Pain. Awful pain. Thank God my wonderful wife was there to support me. After a few minutes I calmed down and called my dad back.

"I'm sorry, Dad. I love you. But I think you are wrong about what you are saying."

"Yeah, okay," my father said. But he was convinced his son was brainwashed. We didn't speak for a long time after that. And it was ten years before I'd see my father again.

Despite the occasional arguments and weird looks, being a sannyasin was easy. Bhagwan asked me to use my new name--- to help me break from the past, which I was eager to do---and to wear orange clothes, and to meditate every day.

Does that sound like the request of a madman to you?

SUNDERAM

It was months before I met any sannyasins. I wandered Houston thinking I was a walking billboard for Rajneesh until one day I saw another orange-clad advertisement walk out of a natural foods store. Turns out he was the director of the Houston meditation center. He was also a University of Houston professor. Through him I met many new sannyasins, including one who was among the most prominent surgeons in the prestigious Texas Medical Center. Bhagwan had a way of drawing in the best people. If you judge him by his fruits, he'd pass inspection.

I started going to meditations and listening to Bhagwan's discourses in the apartment that belonged to the center director. Bhagwan's meditations, for the most part, are extremely active.

The most famous original meditation is called "Dynamic." Most people don't get through the hour-long, bootcamp-like meditation unless they fudge.

The first 10 minutes of Dynamic has you doing cathartic breathing. This is wild. You stand and breathe like a maniac who can't get air. Do this with 15 people in a small room and you get snot all over you. But it really awakens your spirit and pumps new energy into your system.

In the second stage you cathart. That means you let your emotional whims guide you. Feel like screaming? Scream your bloody head off. Wanna cry? Flood the floor. Need to beat a pillow? Go to it. Anything goes in this 15-minute opportunity to cleanse yourself. Observers like this stage because they get to witness craziness at its finest.

The third 10 minutes has you holding your hands straight up to the sky (or ceiling) and jumping up and down, yelling "HOO!" as you land on your feet. It's exhausting. It's a Rambo approach to bliss, and I think Bhagwan was inspired by the Sufis when he created this part. Else he was simply in a cruel mood. It's incredibly difficult (for me, anyway) to do this segment. You really have to override your mind---which is telling you to "STOP!" every time you say "HOO!"

Suddenly we are told to "STOP!", to freeze right where we are. Imagine it. You're jumping up and down and sweating and yelling "HOO!" and wherever you are---freeze. No movement. Nothing. The idea is to look within. Observe. Witness yourself. I'm sure the great Russian teacher Gurdjieff inspired Bhagwan on this one. If you put down your hands or try to relax, you fall back into auto-pilot and you are no longer aware of yourself. So for 10 minutes, you are a statue. My experience with this meditation has been the most fruitful right here, in this fourth stage. Everything preceding leads to the insights you get right here.

Finally, for the last 10 minutes, you dance. You celebrate by moving, swaying, leaping, laughing, whatever feels like a celebration to you. And believe me, after almost an hour of this meditation, you are very willing to celebrate its end.

Dynamic wasn't popular in our weekly meditation gatherings. You can see why. It's far too strenuous and exhausting. And being with 15 people after doing Dynamic is like being in a locker room after a football game. It's not comfortable for anybody.

On my own I would do a meditation called "Mandala." It began with 15 minutes of jogging in place. I believed it was a way to handle two issues with one technique---I got my meditation hour over with AND I got an aerobic work-out. I thought it was pretty enlightened thinking on my part.

Bhagwan believed anything could be a meditation. The requirement was simply your awareness. There's a semi-funny Zen story about a monk in a monastery who asked the man in charge, "Can I smoke while I pray?"

The head monk says, "No way! Praying is sacred! No smoking!"

The next day this same inquiring monk was outside smoking a pipe when the chief monk walked by. The young monk stopped the elder and asked, "Sir, can I pray while I smoke?"

"Of course!" beamed the older monk. "You can pray while doing anything."

Bhagwan was like that. He'd be the first to say you can meditate while smoking. Or eating. Or doing anything else. "Be a witness to it," was a common phrase of his. "Go deeply into it."

So every week a group of Houston disciples and curiosity seekers would do a Bhagwan meditation of some sort. We'd do a more relaxed meditation---Bhagwan had hundreds to choose from---and then we'd listen to our master speak. After a couple hours, we'd hug, exchange small talk, and leave.

It was never enough for me. I thought Bhagwan deserved better and I thought his disciples could do more. And I never liked the center director. Bhagwan had a way of magically connecting people who didn't get along. Call it what you will, disciples were always ending up with other disciples they had personality problems with. Egos bashed. Arguments ensued. Bhagwan probably sat in Poona and roared with laughter. Since his goal was to destroy the ego, he no doubt loved seeing all these egos butting heads.

Anyway, I started my own center. I wrote to Bhagwan and told him what I was up to. I had to write twice before I got another tan envelope in the mail. The center name was to be called "Sunderam Rajneesh Meditation Center." I was to be the director.

My ego loved it. The other center leader's ego hated it. But more disciples liked me than liked him, and my center blossomed.

I held twice-weekly meditations, had monthly introductions to Bhagwan, arranged pot-luck dinners and garage sales, rented a space in a big house for group events, brought to Houston best-selling author Shakti Gawain for a workshop, created a major event---with the help of the Houston surgeon---to introduce Bhagwan to professional people (hundreds came), and I brought in some of the master's own chief disciples and well-known group leaders.

Of course, Bhagwan's groups and group leaders are a whole separate subject. They were as controversial as the master himself. In them, you experienced life in its rawest---and sometimes most dangerous---form.

BROKEN ARMS, BLOODY NOSES

Bhagwan used to tell a story about a seeker who discovered a mysterious tribe on the top of a mountain. When the seeker stumbled across this group, he was stunned. The group was dancing, yelling, crying, screaming, beating each other, fornicating, drinking, eating--- you name it, this group was into it. It was probably like glimpsing into hell.

The seeker turned and fled this insane group.

Years later, out on another expedition in search of truth, the same seeker visited the same tribe at the top of the same mountain. Only now everyone was sitting in silence. And every person had a look of peace.

The seeker wanted to join this group. He sat down with the meditating tribe. But he couldn't sit still. His mind troubled him. While everyone else sat in bliss, the seeker was uneasy. He'd scratch his knee, shift his position, think wild thoughts, imagine devilish events. It didn't take long for the seeker to say the hell with it all and leave the mountain top.

Bhagwan said time and time (and time) again, his whole purpose was to bring us to a state of meditation. But, he would add, you can't meditate right now. Your mind is too full of poison. You have to clear yourself of the garbage before you can still your mind.

So, like the group on the mountain top who ranted and raved and looked pretty strange, we disciples of Bhagwan began our own cleansing process. Dynamic, of course, was a meditation devised to help us dump our emotional and mental baggage. But that was only an hour long. What we needed was something more intense which lasted longer.

We got it, too. Bhagwan's groups became known for their no-holds approach to growth. He attracted some of the most respected therapists in the world, people from Esalen and England, Switzerland and Germany, and Bhagwan gave these leaders freedom. The encounter groups were often so intense that arms were broken. Yet no one---that I know of---ever complained. They willingly signed up for the groups and, scared as they might be, willingly went through them.

Austin had a larger and more active Rajneesh Meditation Center than Houston. It was there that I did my first sannyasin encounter group. Though I had been to Geetam, Bhagwan's large desert oasis, and had done many small groups there, Austin was a longer and more intense experience. I'll never forget it.

For some odd reason the two-day event was held the day after Christmas. This alone upset my wife, as I had to leave Christmas night, and the group began for me because I had to encounter her.

She didn't take it well and spent most of the time I was away drinking and wondering what her husband was doing. The rumors of free sex had reached her too.

Knowing that anything goes in a Rajneeshee group made me nervous. And I tried to hide it, which made me extremely uptight.

There were 30 people in the group. We sat around and let things happen. The group leaders would look right into you and say nothing. This was uncomfortable. You'd wonder if they could read your mind. Then you'd assume they could and you'd open your mouth and reveal yourself. And once you opened your mouth, you were prey for the group.

During one especially intense scene, my nose bled. I wasn't hit, but the energy in the room was so thick, and I was working so hard to keep my fears inside, that something broke and blood dripped down my face. But I didn't try to stop it. I was too wrapped up watching the scene before me.

A young man, a new disciple who still couldn't pronounce Bhagwan's name, was on all fours in the middle of the room. He was bare-chested and his wooden mala swayed from his chest. On his right was the biggest man in the group, holding the disciple in place. On his left was the second biggest man in the group, holding the other side of the disciple. In front of this pinned disciple was the center group leader. The leader was taunting the disciple.

"Your wife slept with two men last night," the leader said. "How do you feel?"

The disciple struggled to get free from the two giants holding him in place.

"Where are those men?" the leader asked. "The men that slept with his wife."

Two men stood. They walked to the group leader.

"Sit here beside me so he can see you two," the leader ordered.

"These men fucked your wife," the leader said. "How do you feel?"

The restrained disciple cried. Then groaned. Something was burning inside him. You could feel it.

"What do you want to do?" the leader asked.

"I want to fucking kill YOU!" and he tried to lunge at the leader. But the huge captors held him in place.

"Feel the anger," the leader said. "Let it go through you."

The disciple, still held down, began a long slow mournful moan that turned into a loud groan and then turned into a scream that made my back arch like a frightened cat's. That scream was thick and deep and seemed to shake the molecules of the house.

At one point the disciple's head was raised to the ceiling and his throat extended in a long curve and he howled like a wolf in the middle of a lonely desert. Everyone felt his anguish. Even now, as I write these words, my skin crawls and my eyes grow moist.

After a few minutes---I'm not sure how long---the man collapsed. My nose was bleeding now. We all watched as the disciple cried and cried. It was pitiful. I wondered why I was in this room. One woman, a non-sannyasin, had already left earlier in the day, when the leader was telling a woman she had to learn how to enjoy the oral sex she gave or she shouldn't do it. Why didn't I leave with her?

As tragic and insane as that experience may seem to you, I want you to know that it transformed the man it happened to. He felt better and looked happier after the bizarre scream. It was as if he had released all the tension and anger he held. Like the tribe on the mountain who had begun their training by catharsis so they could later sit in peace, this disciple needed to dump his pain about his wife's infidelity before he could relax.

But what a way to relax!

There were other unusual instances in Bhagwan's groups, of course. I can still see one attractive female disciple lying in the middle of the hard wooden floor, thirty disciples around her, while the center leader masturbated her. At first I didn't know what he was doing. She was clothed and I assumed he was doing some sort of "energy work" on her. Well, he was. But it wasn't until I saw her squirming and heard her moaning that I realized she was being led to her own intense release.

Again, Bhagwan's groups were designed to lead to inner peace.

If someone was plagued with a recurring image to do something, Bhagwan or his group leaders would say "Go to it!" so you could get it out of your system. This sort of freedom of expression, as you can imagine, got a lot of disciples in trouble.

Despite the insanity in these groups, sanity was usually the result of them. In a paradoxical way the madness led to peace. Encounter groups were popular in the '60s and are still done today. But none of them gave such complete freedom---nearly a license to kill---as did the groups sanctioned by Bhagwan. You have to wonder why. Was Bhagwan just being controversial? Highly unlikely. India already regarded him as their country's most notorious leader. Was Bhagwan intentionally testing his people? Not likely. His disciples wore orange clothes and a mala (the string of wooden beads with a locket of Bhagwan). Anyone who did that in the face of public scorn proved his love for the master.

I believe Bhagwan was a super-psychologist. It's no accident that he drew professional therapists. Bhagwan had the ability to look right past your mask and see into your game---as well as to see your essence and bring it out. Like Ken Wilber, the author of **No Boundary** and other brilliant books on eastern-western psychology and spirituality, Bhagwan knew that the different paths to growth were not contradictory but complimentary. I used to wonder who was right, Freud or Jung? Bhagwan helped me understand that those two psychologists, as well as all the others available, were simply rungs on a ladder. Most of us believed Bhagwan was at the top of the ladder looking down. And for that reason I think that there was an overall divine purpose for going through such intense encounter groups.

After all, Hemingway said a broken arm is stronger after it's healed.

And Lord knows I was able to breathe better after the blood came out of my nose.

OREGON

I never saw Bhagwan in India. Two weeks before my plane was to leave, Bhagwan disappeared. For nearly a year, no one knew where he was. No one would tell, anyway.

Bhagwan had gone into silence. He was no longer speaking, just sitting and radiating his essence. I accepted his silence but was disappointed that he wasn't available. Where'd he go? What was he up to? What do I tell everyone?

Suddenly, Bhagwan showed up. He had been ill, we were told, and he was recovering in a mansion in New Jersey. But more exciting than that, Bhagwan's entire movement was being relocated to a giant piece of land in central Oregon. It was to be called Rancho Rajneesh.

This is where the trouble began.

First, Bhagwan was advised to make his movement a religion. That's when "Rajneeshism" was born. Second, Bhagwan chose the most conservative state in the country to call home, and this angered just about everyone in Oregon. Third, Bhagwan put Ma Anand Sheela in charge, and that may have been his biggest mistake.

I visited Bhagwan twice in Oregon. The first time was a major event. Thousands came from all over the world. Bhagwan was in silence, but seeing him---for the first time in my life---was incredible. I felt his love, his peace, as if it were in the air and there for me to pick up. And when Bhagwan went on his daily drives over the dusty roads, he rode with his foot on the brake so he could look right at each one of his disciples. I remember feeling giddy and laughing joyously right after he would drive by.

Because I was a center director, one night I was given a seat right in front of the master. It was an amazing night. There was thunder and lightning and the threat of a storm. But when Bhagwan appeared, all calmed down. What an entrance! I sat before him, in silence, watching him watch me. It felt healing. I somehow felt like a calm charge was vibrating from him and into me. I don't think I ever saw anyone more centered in my entire life. Bhagwan sat before this crowd, with me in the front row, as if he were a majestic king from a foreign historic time. It would have made a great movie.

That same night I laughed for hours. I couldn't sleep. I was high on life. I wandered the cool night with a dear friend and we laughed uncontrollably. He was laughing more because of me than because of his own inner tickling. Bhagwan used to say his message was "life, love and laughter." I heard his message in some unspoken way that night. I couldn't stop laughing.

There was a television news show about Bhagwan once where the interviewer was standing in the midst of a group of sannyasins, mike in hand, asking questions to anyone who would answer.

"You all are laughing all the time. What's the joke?" he asked.

The crowd exploded in laughter. I laughed out loud, too, as I watched the TV show. The grand joke is life, and Bhagwan's people were enjoying the show.

I had a sore throat the day after my marathon laughing, but it was worth it.

The second time I visited Bhagwan's home was pure hell. Sheela, Bhagwan's fiery little personal assistant, had been given more control over the ranch, and things were falling apart. I wanted to leave the very day I arrived. After landing in Portland, I had to take a four-hour bus ride to the ranch. As I soon as we got off the bus, we were herded into a building and searched. Bhagwan was never into drugs as he said they clouded awareness, but apparently some disciples thought otherwise. So everyone was searched and trained dogs sniffed our luggage. Then we were led to a room with chairs set up in classroom style. There we were told about AIDS and other sexually transmitted

42

diseases. We were taught how to use preventive measures, and were told that Bhagwan wanted everyone to use gloves and condoms and to be "meditative" in sexual practice.

I didn't like the feel of any of this. And it didn't get any better. The near-desert atmosphere of the ranch had my bald head burned red and my Italian cheeks getting chapped. When I tried to buy a hat or lip balm, they were sold out. When supplies were restocked, they charged eight or nine times the going price.

The first time I was at the ranch I felt cared for. The food was excellent, and there were water stations every half mile. But this time around the food was late, and lousy. And the water stations were dry and never refilled. More than once I thought I was going to collapse from the heat. It wasn't fun.

And now Bhagwan, who was protected at all times by body guards with machine guns, was talking again. He had come out of silence and was back into his morning discourses. And he was boring. He spent a lot of time insulting politicians and gossiping.

And he spoke for not one hour, or two hours, but sometimes three hours or more. It was hell on my rear. Some disciples rationalized the event by saying Bhagwan uses whatever he can to hold us in his presence so we can feel his energy. Well, it didn't work with me. I wanted out.

But leaving wasn't easy. Rancho Rajneesh, a 100,000-acre property, was thirty miles from the nearest city. That's a long walk in the desert without water while carrying your stuff. And the city was so small there were no taxis or planes. And it was a four-hour ride from Portland.

So I hung around until my week was up and it was time for me to leave. I did a few workshops, sat in on a few morning discourses, went to a funeral for a disciple who had drowned in a nearby river, went on a bicycle ride, got a nice tan, and so on.

43

But there was no escaping the ugly aura surrounding Bhagwan. By now he was in all the papers. Even "60 Minutes" had come to do a story on him. There was talk of building caves on the ranch to protect some chosen disciples from nuclear annihilation, which Bhagwan said was definitely about to happen. There were rumors of sannyasins poisoning near-by townspeople, organizing into terrorist groups, and beating up non-sannyasins.

Some said Sheela ordered disciples to drug the "street-people" who were collected nationwide and dropped on Bhagwan's ranch. That pseudo-effort to help the homeless---a campaign that got the Ranch front-page publicity in every major newspaper---was nothing more than a con to win political votes, I was told by disciples who lived on the ranch at that time. It was just a show. Once the homeless arrived in Rajneeshpuram, they were forgotten. Most left. Or tried to. They soon learned that walking out of the ranch wasn't easy. You weren't stopped, but you weren't given any rides either.

I found this all of this hard to believe. I had never met ANY sannyasins who wanted to hurt people, drug people, kill people or mislead people. My entire experience with Bhagwan's disciples, including my year as director of his Houston center, was a pleasant one. An exciting one, even. And the people I met were all loving and supportive. Some of the best friends I ever had.

Still, SOMETHING was happening at the Ranch. And I didn't like it. And I couldn't believe I was a part of it. Me, an intelligent, college-educated, middle-class young man, involved with the most controversial guru of this century?!

One morning, right after Bhagwan's discourse, I happened to turn around and I was facing Bhagwan's car.

And he was in it.

And it was coming right at me.

No telling how I managed to be there, especially when ten thousand other people were crawling all over each other to see Bhagwan, but there we were. The car pulled up alongside me and stopped. Bhagwan was in the back seat, by the window, looking at me. He reached up and put his hand on the window. I reached down and put my hand on the outside of the same bullet-proof window. Then he put his hands together and namaste'd to me. I put my hands in the same prayer position and acknowledged him, as well.

And then I was being pushed away by the crowd, and Bhagwan's car was again moving.

I had looked into my master's eyes. I did not see hate or evil. I saw love.

Could this man, the one with the peaceful look and alive eyes, be the same man in charge of fascist disciples? There had even been rumors that the real Bhagwan died in India years ago, that this one in Oregon was an impostor. Could it be?

I also wondered if you could have enlightenment and then lose it. If all the accusations and problems at the ranch were true, and if Bhagwan knew about it and did nothing, or worse yet, encouraged it, then he not only was not enlightened, he was insane.

But who can say for sure? Every disciple has his own interpretation of the facts. A friend of mine---a disciple who divorced his wife over Bhagwan---said Bhagwan had had a "satori" experience. Nothing more. He says Bhagwan had a glimpse of enlightenment and due to the master's gift for gab and his great intellect, he was able to convince hundreds of thousands of intelligent people that he was an awakened being. Is that possible, too? Were we really all that blind?

"Bhagwan fell back into his ego in Oregon," my friend said. "He blew it."

No argument there.

TRUST LIFE

The Ranch fell apart soon after that. Sheela was arrested for embezzlement, attempted murder and who knows what else. Rajneesh was arrested, too, and after jail and a trial, he was deported. For a long time he wasn't permitted to land anywhere.

Every major country said you can refuel your plane but you can't stay. Bhagwan eventually went back to Poona, India, and stayed there until he died.

People still ask me why I was ever with Bhagwan.

"I learned trust," I usually say. "Bhagwan used to say let go and I'll handle everything. Not to worry. All is well. I did let go. I did trust. And I learned that life itself will take care of me. I learned that Bhagwan didn't know me from Adam, but that he knew if I let go, whoever I was, life would guide me along."

But that trust was a two-edged sword. Trusting Bhagwan released me from the struggle to control my life and taught me that life is protective and supportive. But mindless trust in Bhagwan also led to pain, confusion, and the end of his empire.

Some people became disciples because of the rumors of free love. Some went to Bhagwan because they wanted more knowledge and he was a highly read, well-educated being. Still others went to Bhagwan because they wanted a new religion to belong to, something unusual and special to attach their egos to. Probably the smallest group of all went to him for his essence. Bhagwan was an enlightened being. But being enlightened doesn't mean you don't make mistakes or drop your human qualities (or inhuman ones). I believe that at heart Bhagwan was a genuine teacher with a true desire to be of service. He pushed our buttons and made us think, only to make us aware of ourselves. He put himself in a dangerous position---many would hate him, many would love him---but his life would never be ignored. Or forgotten.

I don't know what happened to Bhagwan in Oregon. All I can do is remember the good that I learned from him and remain grateful that I wasn't more involved with him. Some people left their families, their husbands or wives, quit work, sold their entire possessions, and completely redirected their lives to be with Bhagwan. I wonder how they are handling it all now that Bhagwan is gone.

I still have Bhagwan's picture on the wall, the one taken the night I sat before him in Oregon. I look at it and am reminded of his basic message:

"Now is the greatest moment. Enjoy!"

Chapter Three

OPTING FOR LIFE
Happiness, the Option Process and Me

Suffering causes unhappiness.

--Buddha

*Take away the beliefs that cause suffering and you
have happiness.*

--Barry Neil Kaufman

OPTION AND ME

Option has been an incredible blessing for me. If nothing
else, it got me out of my orange clothes.

I was brought up in a Catholic family. My mother often read
stories from the Bible to me when I was a child. I remember how
fascinated I was by their color and wisdom. Somehow I made a

decision at that time to live by the highest truth. For then, I believed Truth to be found in the Catholic Church.

But there were too many changes. For a while we were told to avoid meat on Fridays. I never knew why. Later we were told meat was okay. I never knew why. When I first attended church the mass was in Latin. Later it was altered to half English, half Latin. Switching the rules made me consider that maybe the great church really didn't know what Truth was, after all. I became a very confused child.

I began to look elsewhere. For a while I liked the Mormons. Baptists were okay but seemed to enjoy frightening people with tales of the "great fire" awaiting below. But all the churches fell short when I realized they were just so many different massive groups supporting so many different belief systems. And to top it off, all these unique leaders in religion, though they hardly ever agreed, all claimed Truth was found in one source: the Bible. Well, the Bible must be as confused as I am, I thought, and I moved on.

For a short period I was an atheist. It was extremely discomforting. To think I was alone in the cosmos, on my own, fighting for my life! The image delighted the macho side of me, but that soon withered in the face of a larger reality. It didn't take much thinking for my adolescent mind to realize we are all dependant on each other. I was never alone in the world and, heaven knows, I never wanted to be. And who was I to say God did not exist? I decided it was wisest to at least believe in the possibility of a deity.

Probably because I feared for my life (myself against the world are tough odds), I began to seek power. First physical, by working out and learning martial arts such as Aikido and Karate; and second mental, by exploring the powers of the mind. Fascinated by hypnosis, telepathy and tales of psychic dominance, I joined an E.S.P. Laboratory and tried to leave my body. I never found the astral plane. I tried to contact the dead, too, hoping someone on the other side had seen God. But I met no one.

Still searching, still seeking, still confused, I stumbled across a book by an Indian guru. Delighted by his wisdom, drawn in by his mesmerizing style, I became a disciple. My Catholic parents were stunned. But through this guru I learned God was the totality of all existence, that God was as much in me as in you, and that Truth was inside. Well, I looked there. At times I felt maybe, just maybe, Truth really was inside me. Was it that peaceful essence I sometimes felt after a meditation? I wasn't sure. The guru said don't worry about it. Life is a mystery and a ridiculous joke, he declared, so enjoy the show!

For seven years, I did. I put on orange clothes and a string of wooden beads to signify my relationship to my master, and I meditated every day. I felt good, but not great. Where's Truth?, I continued asking. The guru said to question everything. That's how you reach Truth, he said. But how do you question? He didn't say. Because certain disciples never questioned what was happening in our circle, because the guru himself did not question his people, major legal battles ensued over alleged crimes of attempted murder and embezzlement. The guru's spiritual world crumbled. And my search for Truth continued.

Onwards through Zen, Taoism, Unity, bizarre cults and new ideas. Tasted all the different psychologies, and found them the new religions of the western world, modern belief systems made to satisfy and understand a new breed of people. I stayed with each psychology as long as I could believe in it. Sooner or later they would be unable to answer one of my questions---like "What is Truth?"---and I would be on my way.

Attended workshops where Nazi-like leaders interrogated me and told me what was wrong with me. That told me a lot about their beliefs, but shed little light on mine.

I always felt terrific at the end of one of these "growth seminars" because I was so glad the ordeal was finally over.

I loved literature and looked for answers there, too. But the biographies of authors told me that most of them were miserable, alcoholic, and had no idea what they were talking about.

Still believing my answers were in books, I continued to devour titles, reading a volume a day at one point. But why did the books conflict so much? Isn't Truth universal, holistic and peaceful? I remember standing in a bookstore, frustrated, surrounded by hundreds of titles, thinking, "These are nothing but belief systems!"

And then, because of a suggestion by Wayne Dyer, I read Barry Neil Kaufman's book *To Love Is To Be Happy With*.

And I discovered Option.

Option? A strange name for a new process of self-discovery. Another belief system? No, it is a way to explore beliefs. Does it work? The books by the Kaufmans chronicled some awesome miracles. Would it work for me?

It was worth a try.

A PLACE FOR MIRACLES

From my journal entry for Sept. 27. Houston:

The flyer advertising the One-Week Option Process Intensive asks, "Imagine that you could begin again, that you could recreate yourself exactly as you want to be. Where would you start?"

I am beginning by registering for that class.

How can I resist? Already familiar with the stunning work of the Kaufmans---through their bestselling books and tapes---I know in my heart that a week of Option could transform my life.

The flyer goes on to say, "Perhaps you'd choose the freedom to be completely happy ... with no limits."

Believing that unlimited happiness would be worth my time and money, I am leaving for the Option Institute tonight......

****

The Option Process is a way to expose the beliefs that fuel unhappiness. Developed by Barry Neil Kaufman, author of *To Love Is To Be Happy With*, *Giant Steps*, *A Miracle To Believe In* and *A Sense of Warning* (among other titles, all of which are required reading in 280 universities), the Option method is a Socratic dialogue process where you and a trained Option mentor converse.

"All" the mentor does, however, is ask you a few basic questions while totally accepting whatever you say. More than anything else, Option is a non-judgmental, completely loving process. The mentor never tells you what to say, think or do. He never judges you. In Option, you are your own best expert and you are always doing the best you can.

Results with the Option Process are amazing, even miraculous. Autistic children become normal, the most famous case being Barry and Suzi Kaufman's own son, Raun, whose story is told in Kaufman's bestselling book, *Son-Rise*, and which was seen by millions in the award-winning TV movie of the same name (which Kaufman also wrote). Cancer patients heal themselves or learn to accept their condition with dignity and love. Suicidal people choose life. Victims of tragic crimes learn to be happy. It is no wonder the Option Institute in Sheffield, Massachusetts, is called "A Place For Miracles."

Option is a lifestyle perspective, a therapeutic technique and an educational alternative. At the heart of the Option Process is the loving and accepting attitude "To love is to be happy with." From there, questions are asked so that the beliefs which cause unhappiness or misery, illness, self-defeating behavior, etc.) can be gently uncovered. Kaufman says Option creates "Happy detectives, sleuthing for the clues (beliefs) of unhappiness...in order to free ourselves to be happier, more self-trusting, and self-empowering in our everyday experience as well as in difficult and challenging situations."

Central to the Option Process are the following concepts:
---Becoming happier is a beautiful (not painful) process.

---We all do the best we can, the best we know how, based on our current beliefs.

---Each of us is our own best expert.

---Questions are not signs of doubt, but opportunities to crystallize what we know.

---Unhappiness is based on a logical system of beliefs, beliefs we can question, change or discard.

---Once we change our beliefs, our feelings and behaviors change easily.

---Happy people are more powerful and effective than unhappy people in getting what they want.

---We love to the extent we are happy.

I recently spent one week at the Kaufmans' 85-acre Option Institute, on a beautiful mountaintop straddling Connecticut and Massachusetts. I went there curious about the Option Process and impressed with the results of Barry and Suzi Kaufman's work. What follows are excerpts from the journal I kept while living the "One-Week Option Intensive."

****

Sept. 28. Option Institute.
When I first arrived here early today I was tired and feeling negative. I was ready to go back to Houston. A three-hour flight,

three-hour drive, a traffic ticket for not wearing a seat belt in the State of New York, getting lost in the Bronx for over an hour---all of this took its toll on me. And why? Because (as I now realize) I chose to allow that. I chose misery.

It wasn't until 7:30 tonight, only a couple hours ago, that it all began to come into focus. Barry Neil Kaufman, founder of this incredibly beautiful home for miracles, author of some of the most inspiring books I have ever read, spoke for two hours on my being here.

Not just MY being here, of course, but why every one of the dozen or so people who arrived today from various parts of the U.S. chose to be here.

"Bears," as Barry likes to be called, asked each of us, "Why are you here, right now, in this room?"

As he pointed out, it is a question you can ask yourself at any time, anywhere. Why are you reading this? Why am I writing this? The question brings us into this moment, and focuses our thoughts on what we want right now. For me, that question lets me know I decide why I am anyplace. With that knowledge comes a certain freedom and power. If I decided to be here, I must also decide everything else for myself. So---what else do I want for me in this (or any) moment?

Bears' two-hour discourse was fascinating. Though we had traveled from as far away as Seattle and as near as Boston, all present listened with wide-eyed excitement as Bears talked about wanting, miracles and being happy.

What I'll say here will seem limp compared to the actual experience. We were invited to be happy now. Not to think about it, but to be it. Right now. Not tomorrow, not after an Option dialogue session, but at this very moment.

Bears said the three-step process for making our week here a happy and successful one was:

---Ask yourself, "Do I want to be happy?" The awareness that "I want to be happy" is the first step in moving toward happiness.

---Ask yourself, "Do I think it is possible?" Acknowledge to yourself that "I can be happy" and you will be free to actually be happy.

---Decide that you want happiness---NOW!

Barry spoke a long time about wanting, about the difference between saying you want something and actually doing something to achieve what you want. He spoke about buying this glorious 100-year-old Option house, how he and his wife Suzi really didn't have the money for the house, that they were in fact over a half million dollars short. But they truly wanted this property. So they made a list of people they knew who might give them donations. Later they made a list of people who might give them loans. The point is, they moved toward their want. They didn't talk. They acted. They didn't listen to people tell them what was or was not possible. Instead, the Kaufmans created a miracle. And the Option Institute was dubbed "A Place For Miracles."

The Kaufmans' healing of their autistic child is another story Bears uses to illustrate his message.

Barry and his wife did not listen to the so-called experts (twelve institutions said Raun was incurable). They instead chose to try something else, something risky and new but in alignment with their wanting the best for their child. They worked with Raun seven days a week, twenty-four hours a day, for more than three years. Today Raun is an above-average teenager with a near genius IQ. (I later met Raun and was impressed with his aliveness and intelligence. He is now an Option mentor at the Institute.)

And Bears told the story about his most popular book, *To Love Is To Be Happy With*. Bears knew he wanted that book published. "If I came to this planet to do anything," he told us, "it was to write that book." Yet fifty-seven publishing houses rejected it. Still, Bears moved on, always going for his desire. He obtained a young, smart agent, changed the title of his book from "You Never Ever Have To Be Unhappy Again" to its present title, and the rest is history. That book continues to out-sell all of Barry's other books. Another miracle!

Bears pointed out that his happiness is not based on having what he wants. He is happy now. And out of that state he chooses what he wants. He is free to have it all.

"Anything is possible to do or have," Bears said. "Reality is simply a construct we erect. We can re-design reality whenever we want and so choose."

Barry then gave us a powerful suggestion on how to be happy right now. "Use everything as an opportunity," Barry said, "to be happy with. You don't like your roommate? Fine. Be happy about it. You're cold? Fine. Be happy with that. You don't need an Option session to give you the insight you think you need to be happy. You can be happy right now. And that is a wonderful opportunity."

So for this week we dozen happiness-seekers share a common goal: we want to be happy now, with whatever is in this "now."

Later, over tea, I overheard a fellow say he didn't understand how having goals or meeting goals could make him happy. "Once I get what I want," he said, "I feel empty until I decide on my next goal."

A retiree from New Orleans, here as a volunteer for six months on a work-study program, explained in his heavy Dutch accent, "You be happy as you go for goals---not because of goals."

Be happy now.

Go for whatever you want.

Sept. 29.
"What do you want to talk about?" Robin asked me as we began a one-hour walk down a beautiful country road. This was my first

Option Process session. I chose my desire to lose weight. Though I have lost ninety pounds in the last year, I still have at least twenty pounds to go and I feel stuck. So for an hour we explored---no, I explored my beliefs about weight control---and "all" Robin did was ask careful questions.

I got in contact with a lot of inner material. I realized I don't really fear going back up to 290 pounds. I also realized that leveling off right now at 200 is what I want. I am taking care of myself. It is a level where I feel okay, for now, and where I can "indulge" somewhat in food without being on a strict diet. After all, I have been dieting for more than a year. Being at my present weight is a break from the long process to reaching my ideal goal weight.

I also explored the struggle I often have over whether to eat or not eat when I face food. Do I want the immediate taste or do I want to be thin? If I eat, it may mean my journey toward my goal is interrupted or slowed down. If I don't eat, I arrive at my goal sooner but miss the immediate sensory gratification. Choosing is sometimes extremely difficult.

Here is a tiny excerpt from my Option session with Robin, a moment in the dialogue that was a real turning point for me:

"I seem to have two conflicting wants," I told Robin. "Wanting the food and wanting to lose weight. It is a tug-of-war inside me to decide which want to pursue."

"Why would you make it so difficult to decide?"

"To strengthen myself," I quickly responded. The answer surprised me too. And then I laughed.

"Why did you laugh?"

"Because I am creating and slaying my own dragons," I replied. "I must actually want the struggle to decide in order to help build the inner me."

That remains a powerful insight into my own behavior. I am creating my own difficulties in order to help me grow. Amazing! And even more incredible is the fact that if I am creating this difficulty, I can also choose not to create it. Losing weight can be as easy as I want it to be.

Later, in the afternoon classroom session, we were asked to divide into groups and then go out and find one thing we all deemed "good" and one thing we all deemed "bad." A sort of philosophical scavenger hunt.

My group decided we could not possibly find anything free of judgment. We knew this game was a set-up. No matter what we brought back, it could be seen as either good or bad, depending on your choice of perception. So we decided to go for a walk and just enjoy that activity. When we went to put our shoes on, one of the ladies in my group, Mary, discovered that someone had left her a pair of shoes that looked like hers but which didn't fit her feet.

"Oh, gosh! That's bad!" Mary said. We all laughed. But then Mary said, "Now I can go barefoot, though, and that's good!" We all laughed again. Mary looked inside the shoes and found a pack of cigarettes. "This is bad," she said. But Carol, another group member, likes to smoke and she said, "That's good!" We were all cracking up by now. Mary then looked inside the pack of cigarettes and found a ten-dollar bill. We all agreed that was good.

The shoe story became our good-bad item for show-and-tell later. It illustrated how we judge events all day, and automatically. What my group concluded is that life, and how you see it, is your decision. The sun shining is just the sun shining. A farmer may see it as good or bad depending on his needs. If he wants rain for his crops, the sunshine is bad. Still, the sun just shines.

Can we lead our lives free of judgment? Just flowing? Bears said, "Happiness is as easy as breathing."

Then why do we even have unhappiness? Bears says there are three main reasons:

1. We use it to motivate ourselves or others.

2. We use it as a sign of our sensitivity and caring.

3. We use it as a threat.

"Unhappiness," Bears said, "is the Queen of our culture."

Sept. 30.

What I've learned today, in my own use of the Option Process, is that what counts most in the process is the attitude: non-judgment of the person you are talking to, and of yourself. The questions are almost useless if I ask them from judgment. On the other hand, any question might work if I ask it with total love.

In one exercise we paired off and one person spoke while the other person did nothing but listen. It is pretty hard to do. When I spoke I found myself seeking clues from my listener so I would know she wasn't bored. We are so used to wanting approval that we try to detect a need and then fill it. Since my listener gave no cue or sign of a need, I felt free to say anything.

As a listener I found it slightly difficult to remain silent. I wanted to interject a thought or ask a question or solve the problem.

But I learned that a certain healing takes place from being with a person nonjudgmentally. I as listener am free to really hear what is being said. I as speaker believe that what I say is being heard and not distorted or rejected.

The Option questions are used to help the person talking discover his or her own thoughts and thinking patterns. The questions cause you to slow down the usually lightning-fast mental process so you can see what you are telling yourself on a below-conscious level.

The first Option question, "What are you unhappy about?", focuses on an issue. "Do you have an example?" and "What do you mean?" are variations of the same question. They are clarifiers, used to help you vividly connect with an area of unhappiness or discomfort.

"Why are you unhappy about that?" is a question that uncovers reasons (beliefs) causing the unhappiness. "Why do you believe that?" or "Do you believe that?" takes you even deeper, helping you unearth the rationale behind the beliefs. Then there is "What are you afraid would happen if you didn't believe that?", another eye-opening question.

As far as I know there is only one statement ever made in the Option Process. It is: "Wanting something and being unhappy about it are two different things."

To me that insight is as powerful as thunder in awakening me. Buddha said our attachments cause suffering. Bears says we don't need to be attached to what we want. Happiness is separate from desire. You can be happy and go for whatever you want.

That's profound! All these years of being told (by very wise spiritual teachers) that what I want is wrong---when in fact it is my very birthright to want! Only when I am attached to my desires do I hurt myself or others. Suzi Kaufman once said, "You can want what you want and still not need it to happen. You don't have to be unhappy if it doesn't happen."

If I am unhappy because I want to lose weight, I can tell myself, "Wanting to lose weight and being unhappy about losing weight are two different things. Why am I unhappy about losing weight?" The Option statement is a clear reminder that I have choice, and an effective tool for opening me to further exploring my beliefs.

It seems too simplistic to say "That's all there is to it," but essentially that IS all there is to the Option questioning process. Provided the questions are asked out of love---if they aren't asked with love the person answering will actually defend his beliefs rather than explore them---you can use them to gently explore why you do what you do. Do you smoke? Overeat? Drink? You are acting on beliefs integrated in your mind a long time ago. The Option Process helps make those unconscious beliefs conscious. Once you discover what you are believing, you are free to choose another way. When you change your beliefs, an Option concept states, your actions naturally change.

Oct. 1.

As I lay in bed this morning I noticed my mind drift and think negative thoughts. I got unhappy about that. I didn't want negative thoughts or to be unhappy about them if I did have them. Then I remembered something Suzi Kaufman said last night. She was asked, "When was the last time you were unhappy?"

Suzi thought for a long time and said she couldn't remember, that whenever the process begins that creates unhappiness she just stops the game and says to herself, "I have a choice. Do I want to be happy or unhappy?" And she chooses happiness.

Suzi illustrated her point with a story about their adopted son, Tao. The child once fell while holding a pencil. The pencil went into his eye and the lead nearly entered his brain. Though most of us would have panicked or been unhappy, Suzi and Bears were calm and happy and did what was needed to be done to help the child. Because they were happy, they were clear enough to see what had to be performed next. And they saved the child.

I thought of all that and realized I could choose to be unhappy or not about my negative thoughts. I decided to be happy about them. That made me smile. Then I thought, "I ought to be able to control the thoughts themselves. Thinking negative is a choice."

But then I thought, "How do you stop thoughts?"

Right then and there the thoughts stopped! I lay on the bed looking at the wall and just seeing it. No thoughts. No judgments. Simply a wonderful open peacefulness and alertness.

Suddenly I began to think again as I began to breathe. It seemed that as my thoughts stopped, so did my breathing. When I began to breathe, I began to think.

Perhaps through thirty years of training I have taught myself that thinking is as natural as breathing. But now I wonder---because I have had a very clear example that I have the power to control my own mind!

Later: To add to what I was saying yesterday, that the listener/mentor's inner being is what counts, that his (or her) accepting, nonjudgmental attitude is what is transformative, I offer this quote from Bernie Siegel's book *Love, Medicine and Miracles*:

"Studies have shown that when you put a janitor in a psychiatrist's office, the patient gets better---as long as the janitor is empathetic."

Caring is the key---but it is a nonattached caring. It occurs to me that caring sometimes means "I want you to feel better." But love means "I accept you as you are."

When I called Marian yesterday it was right after my second Option session. I was feeling quite wonderful inside. But she was very nervous and nearly hyperventilating due to her concern over a job offer and some possible complications. I allowed her to feel what she felt. I didn't push her or guide her or try to change her. I simply stayed with her, letting her say what she wanted. In only a few moments her voice calmed, her breathing returned to normal, and she began to ask me questions about my week here. It was as though my calmness calmed her.

Clarity, it seems, is contagious.

Don't judge yourself or another in a dialogue and you will pretty much be doing the Option Process. The attitude---"to love is to be happy with"---is the entire key to success.

Sometimes it is hard for me to realize that just being with someone is miraculous. If I listen, really listen, then I am there for that person. If I try to lead the conversation in any way, I am in effect saying "I know better than you." In Option, the individual is his or her own best expert.

Oct. 2.
Here are some ways to live a happy life:

-- Don't make unhappiness the enemy. Unhappiness is a strategy we have learned to help us survive. It is a choice, and it is okay to choose unhappiness if that is what you want. Don't get unhappy about unhappiness. Accept it, too.

-- Be a "Good-Finder." If you still want to judge the things you see in the world, then judge everything as good.

Any time you are grateful, you are happy. Look around right now and find something, anything, that you feel grateful for. It can be a tree, this paper, the sun. Anything! When you are grateful, you open yourself to happiness.
-- Be in the present. You are never unhappy in the total now. In the present moment, everything is fine. Unhappiness is future- and past-oriented.

That last suggestion reminds me of a quote by Hank Williams, Jr., "If you aren't happy, you're missing a great opportunity."

Oct. 3.
Your happiness isn't dependent on having or getting anything. You can be happy now. An Option saying states, "Happy people tend to get what they want, and when they don't, they want what they get."

Oct. 4.

One of the best "shortcuts" to happiness is to feel grateful. Tonight we spent four hours feeling grateful. It was awesome. Each member of the group took a turn at saying what he or she was thankful for from this week's experience. When it came to me, I couldn't contain myself. I was passionate in my gratitude. I told Bears his work has continued to open inner doors for me, that his Sunday night lecture sent me flying, that it was an incredible gift to meet him, that I would continue to send my support to him, and that I would return for further training in the Option Process.

After everyone had shared their feelings and gratitude, we stood and sang the old song, "All I want from you is forever to remember me as loving you." Before we began to sing we chose partners. Bears bee-lined to me. It was an authentic acknowledgment of his appreciation of me, and mine of him. And, finally, we all hugged one another. It was an incredibly powerful experience.

I feel honored, touched, grateful, healed, loved, rejuvenated and amazed. If anyone asks me what I did these past few days to feel so great, what can I possibly say? That I shared moments with a dozen wonderful people? That we played games, listened to stories, talked, ate, slept, and felt very, very happy? Words don't describe the very real miracle that I have experienced here at the Option Institute. It is truly "A Place For Miracles."

****

THE MAN WHO BECAME GOD

In grade school I created a simple exhibit for the Science Fair. There wasn't anything different about my project. It had been done many times before. And it didn't win any prizes. But I'm glad I made the thing anyway. That science project, done more than two decades ago, helps me explain the inner workings of the Option Process.

You probably saw my exhibit. Or one like it. It was a flat wooden board with two rows of colorful bird pictures on the top half and two rows of bird names on the bottom half.

Beside the board were two screwdrivers. You placed one screwdriver on a screw below the photo of a bird. You placed the other one on a screw below the name of a bird. If the bird and name matched, a light went on.

That's what I see happening in Option. We explore our beliefs until something connects and a light comes on. The light DOES come on, too. You can see it in a person's eyes. In their face. In the warm, luminous glow that suddenly appears around a person when they have an insight into themselves that frees them from a past belief.

My science project is my analogy for Option. You ask questions and accept answers until the two click and a light comes on. Now let me share with you my most memorable Option Process experience. It all began one evening about a year ago, when I developed a strong desire to attend the hottest seminar around . . .

I met John at a Firewalk. The fact that I walked over red-hot coals isn't as important as my meeting John that night. The event was the beginning of our friendship.

We met for lunch a few days after the Firewalk. I was interviewing John to gather information for an article I wanted to write. But as our discussion grew deeper and our personal sharings expanded, I learned he was in the middle of a personal inner struggle. He was being pulled in two very different directions, one way by his ego, the other way by the divinity within him. His body was becoming a battlefield for this psychological tug-of-war, and he was paying a heavy price. His happiness, his health, his marriage and his future were all at stake.

John didn't know about the Option Process. But he did know I cared for him, and that he could tell me anything. We continued to meet and had already met several times when, one cold day last

Winter, we began a spontaneous Option session---one that would dramatically change the course of his life.

We met at a university cafeteria south of Houston. Though it was noon and the place was crowded, it was as if no one else was there but John and me. Though I know people came and went, and some even overheard our unusual conversation, I never looked away from John. I was totally there for him. His face showed a man twisted by inner rumblings. His body was tight. Tense. He was afraid to let go. Even his hands were fists.

I admit I was afraid. John is tall and powerful. And he has a black belt in karate. I was very aware of those facts as I watched the bottled aggression in him move around. I knew he might lash out and crush my face. But I also knew I loved him. I also trusted the situation. Somehow, some way, I knew it was all okay. Even if he hit me, I could accept it.

I didn't want that, of course, but I could accept it. And that fact gave me a powerful sense of freedom.

I don't recall all of what John and I said. I remember being in awe of his openness, at how easily and quickly he shed his negative beliefs. And I remember seeing his inner light come on several times as we explored his beliefs. I still delight in that memory---in seeing his face change and lighten as his mental wiring created new connections.

I'll try to recreate some of our dialogue:

What was John feeling? Afraid. *Afraid of what?* Of letting the God-Self (his words) take over his life. *What was the God-Self?* His inner divinity, he said, the goodness of the universe. *Why was he afraid to let goodness take over his life?* The energy of God would fuel the bad in him as well as the good.

What did he mean? His face tightened. His eyes hardened. His breathing was labored. Something was going on in him. I feared he might explode. But I reminded myself to trust the process. I relaxed. A little.

John began to tell me about his past. He had done things as a youth he'd never forgiven himself for. *Like what?*

He told me. *Why hadn't he forgiven himself?* He thought he needed to be punished. *Why?* So he wouldn't be bad anymore. *Did he want to be bad?* No. *Then why did he punish himself?* He smiled. An inner light came on. He knew he didn't need to punish himself to keep from doing something he didn't want to do anyway.

So why was he afraid to let go to his divinity? The God-energy would feed the weeds as well as the flowers, he said. *What was God-energy?* Goodness. *What were the weeds?* Badness. *Did he believe goodness would feed badness?* No, he said, of course not!

And then John changed. All the inner lights came on. His body softened, relaxed. His breathing was deeper, fuller. His eyes---I swear it---actually seemed to change color. John was no longer John. And the change was so obvious that an onlooker in the cafeteria asked if John was okay.

Over the last year John has gone through amazing changes. His personal-growth seminars---which had been done at no charge for small groups---are now drawing crowds and paying him big money. John has been given an office, a seminar space, and a wonderful job at a hospital. He is now invited to give talks to numerous groups. He has a growing list of regular clients who come to him for counseling. And his relationships with himself, his wife, and everyone else seem relaxed and happy.

How did Option help him? As John later told me, his beliefs needed restructuring. My questions helped him touch screwdrivers and screws (remember my science project) until the lights came on. In other words, we cleared out the past negative beliefs so he was free to be whatever he wanted to be---and for John, the next step was inner transformation.

John is still John, of course. He doesn't have wings, he doesn't bring the dead back to life, and his wife will tell you that he is still very human. But there is a certain wholeness and energy about John that lets you know his inner war is over. He is at peace. He is happy. And isn't that what Godhood and enlightenment are all about?

John's metamorphosis is a wonderful example of how Option works. You use an Option dialogue to explore the beliefs preventing you from being happy. Once you are happy, you are better able to choose what you want for yourself. And once you know what you want, you are able to begin to create it. And that's when you begin to create miracles.

THE POWER OF BELIEF

On a recent PBS television special James Burke, author of *The Day The Universe Changed*, explained and proved that we have always interpreted life in accordance with our beliefs. Whether you are a Buddhist or a Western scientist, you "fit" everything you experience into your own particular model of reality. For a couple thousand years we knew for a fact that the sun revolved around the earth. Now we know better. Or do we? Will another Copernicus soon appear to alter our present beliefs about reality?

Look into the world of medicine. In the early 1800s, a favorite treatment was "bleeding"---a term which aptly describes the therapy. Many patients, including George Washington, probably died sooner than necessary because of this "cure" for their pains. Why did Doctors open veins and let out blood? Because, of course, they believed it would help. Why don't we "bleed" patients today? Because we now believe it won't help.

Consider the famous "placebo effect." Take two people with the same illness. Give one an authentic medication and the other a sugar-pill. Both patients will heal in tune with their beliefs concerning the "medicine." Andrew Weil, author of *Health And Healing*, has stated (along with other scholars) that the entire history of medicine may simply be the history of the placebo.

Anthony Robbins, in **Unlimited Power**, mentions a schizophrenic woman who was diabetic while one personality and perfectly healthy as the other personality. One of her selves believed she was ill, so her body produced that illness. The other self believed she was well, and her body produced that effect.

Hypnosis is another example of how beliefs control reality. When I was a teenager I experimented with hypnosis. I placed a suggestive friend of mine in a light trance and told him his left hand would feel an ice cube touch it. I then placed a lit match against that hand. He did not burn (lucky for me). Instead he grinned and said, "That's cold!"

Wayne Dyer offers other evidence for the power of belief. In **Pulling Your Own Strings,** Dyer writes about a 1960s experiment where a teacher was given the I.Q. test results for his new students. They were not all legitimate   scores, however. Some of the I.Q. figures were in fact numbers taken off the students' lockers. At the end of the year everyone performed as well as their "I.Q." results had predicted. The students with higher locker numbers scored higher than the students with lower locker numbers. Everyone believed in the I.Q. scores---and created their own realities based on what they believed.

When I was in high school I read and re-read Claude   Bristol's classic book, **The Magic Of Believing**. Because of Bristol's masterpiece I believed I could do anything---even beat my father in a hot game of ping-pong.

My Dad could easily defeat me in that indoor sport. But after reading Bristol's book a few times I convinced myself I could win against my Dad. I remember spending a lot of time in a chair with my eyes closed, visualizing myself playing perfect table-tennis. When I believed I could do it, I challenged my father. Always ready to defeat his son, he agreed to play.

But Dad didn't know how prepared I was. Not only did I beat him in that game of ping-pong, I won every game we played that day!

THE REAL MIRACLE

I regard Option and the work of the Kaufmans as breath-taking. I see that most people live their lives in a box of beliefs. We're never aware of these beliefs. We just call what happens to us "life." But what happens to us is based on our beliefs. Recently I read an interview with Bears where he said "Beliefs ARE reality." If that's the case, and I believe it is, then you can change your reality by changing your beliefs. And Option is just the tool to do it.

Fact is, there is a wonderful Option counselor in the San Diego, California, area by the name of Mandy Evans who is helping people change their past by exploring beliefs. It seems the past, present and future are all plastic. We can mold them into what we want by changing our beliefs. Mandy has been doing Option more than twenty years and leads a transformative workshop called "Beyond The Past" where she helps people reframe their past.

"It's not the past that hurts us," Mandy once told me, "it's the beliefs we've created about the past. Those beliefs are open to question."

The way Mandy questions beliefs is through Option. The goal isn't to change the beliefs, she explains in her little guidebook, ***Emotional Options***, but to simply look at them. "Option is an opportunity to question feelings and beliefs in the most loving, accepting, constructive way that we can muster," she explained to me.

It's a little frustrating to me that more people don't know about Option. So many people are unhappy. So many people are suffering. So many people are not satisfied with their lives. So many people are blaming the past for their current situation. Yet it's all pointless and needless. No doubt we are all doing the best we can, but I now know we can do better and certainly be happier with whatever we do. You now know this, too. Option has shown me that miracles are possible. No matter what you have in your life, or what you face, you have the power to transform it. The choice, as always, is yours.

That, to me, is a very real miracle. And it is the gift inherent in the wonderful Option Process.

Chapter Four

THE HEALING VISION OF MEIR

I wanted to meet Meir Schneider before I ever read his book. The brochure about *Self-Healing: My Life and Vision* said it was by a man who had healed himself of blindness. I was fascinated. I love true stories of people who overcome "hopeless" situations. Meir had been diagnosed as incurable. He was even given a certificate of blindness by the Israeli government. But here he was. Not only writing a book and helping others to see again, but he was also driving through the streets of California with a non-restricted California Drivers License.

Yes, I had to meet this man.

I found Meir's book remarkably candid and inspiring. There was more philosophy than exercises, and that surprised me. I had expected to find a book full of "eye exercises" and breathing techniques. There was little, almost none, of that. I called Meir at his San Francisco office. It was July 4th, Independence Day, when we first chatted. He was easy to talk to. Because he was born in the USSR in 1954, and raised in Israel, I thought his speech might be hard to understand. It wasn't. He was very clear, articulate, and passionate. I liked him at once.

He arranged to meet me here in Houston. He was already heading out to Cape Cod for a long-awaited vacation. He simply rerouted his flight so he could have a few hours with me at Intercontinental Airport. I agreed to it, of course. I was extremely excited about meeting him and began to prepare by reading everything I could find on Meir. He made this research easier by sending me a large package with copies of articles on him.

ABOUT THE MAN

I learned Meir was born to Jewish parents who were deaf. That had to be an impossible situation. A blind youth with deaf parents? My God. It's staggering to think about. Meir had cataracts on both eyes and suffered from glaucoma and nystagmus (involuntary eye movement). He was operated on in Poland in 1959. He later moved to Israel and went through another four operations. By then Meir's lenses were so ravaged he was declared legally and incurably blind.

Meir learned to read with the Braille method. After reading three books a week this way, he met a youth who taught him some special exercises. The exercises were from the work of Dr. Bates, a controversial turn-of-the-century American ophthalmologist. After 18 months of "sunning" and "palming" and other Bates exercises, Meir could see.

Word of Meir spread throughout Israel. He quickly became a sought-after authority on healing. Though he is still considered questionable here, he is looked at as a national hero in his home country. So far Meir has helped more than 3,000 people world-wide cure themselves of various ailments. He doesn't stop at vision problems. He has helped folks with sclerosis, arthritis, polio, multiple sclerosis, and even muscular dystrophy. And he has a success rate greater than ninety percent.

Meir is dedicated to his mission. He has worked 15 years and has put in 40,000 hours of hands-on experience. And he works ten to twelve hours a day, every day, seeing clients at his Center For Self-Healing in San Francisco, which he started in 1977.

MEETING MEIR

I recognized Meir when he walked off the plane. There were about five people around him, all wearing glasses. Apparently Meir had been telling his success story to the passengers near him in first-class. I admired him for openly sharing himself with strangers. He wasn't missing any chances to help people or to promote his book.

Meir is about 5'8" and maybe 160. He has dark hair and a slightly stocky build. I noticed he blinked his eyes a lot and he seemed to have trouble focusing. For a moment I wondered if he could REALLY see me.

We shook hands. He was easy to be with. He asked me about my life, my work, and my family. He seemed genuinely interested in me, which is very unusual with most people I write about. Most simply want to talk about themselves. Meir treated me as a wonderful new friend in his life.

I asked when his flight left so I knew how much time we had to talk. He felt around in his pockets until he found his ticket. But he had trouble reading it. He stared at it for a long time before giving it to me. I felt like I was helping a little boy read directions home. I wondered if Meir was like this when he was behind the wheel of his car.

We walked thru the terminal and went to the cafeteria. I set up my tape player and started to ask questions. Meir leaned back and responded in a warm, sincere, yet intensely focused manner.

"You were born blind and had five operations--"

"I went through five operations and a sixth exploratory operation," Meir interrupted.

"And that broke the lenses of your eyes, right?"

"Yes. Physically I shouldn't be able to see at all."

"Yet you can," I said. "You were declared legally blind. You were told it was hopeless. Yet you persisted. Why?"

"You know the old saying 'Pain leads to growth'? For me it was painful not to be able to do what other people could do, to be an exception. What happened to me is that I met a sixteen-year-old genius. He told me to take my glasses off. I could see light and shadow with them. He told me to see light and shadow without them. See them fuzzier. Start there. That's the first thing he taught me, see what you see, possess your eyes. Blind people eventually become more blind because they aren't expected to see. Just because somebody has one percent of vision, that one percent shouldn't be dismissed."

I was impressed with Meir's reasoning. And I was in awe being with him. I greatly admired him.

"I always understood blindness to be total blackness, total nothingness," I said. "But you're saying there are degrees of seeing."

"Right! Exactly!" Meir said with a burst of enthusiasm. "And ninety percent of blind people do see something, even those who have guide dogs."

"Can you give me an example of what you're saying?"

"A friend of mine came here from Austria recently. She's blind and has a guide dog. She had non-functional vision. Yet she had a sense of colors and she could sense some objects---she did not know this actually until I met with her. Her vision was so non-functional that she didn't know what she could do.

"In Austria blind people wear a yellow tag on their arm," Meir continued. "She was in a supermarket, shopping. I taught her to move toward what she could see, and she slowly moved to the yogurt. She had a sense of its boundaries---she might not see it the way you see it, but she had a sense of its shape. She extended her hand, took the yogurt, and placed it in her cart. An old woman standing behind her suddenly screamed, 'You have no right to wear that yellow tag when you can see!'"

That's a powerful story," I said. "So you taught this woman to be aware of what she could in fact already do but didn't know she could do?"

"Yes!"

"So you're saying, work with what you can see, develop that?"

"Or with what you can hear, if you're having hearing problems, or with what you can smell, if that's a problem, or with the amount of movement you can make if you have paralysis."

"And that creates change?" I asked.

"The biggest difference between me and physical therapists is that they'll say, 'Your arms work so let's work with your arms.' I'm saying to hell with that. If you can work your arms already, fine. Let's see if something moves in your legs, something of insignificance, but let's see if it moves. You'd be amazed at how much movement most wheelchair patients have, and they don't even know it. It was never encouraged."

"Were you encouraged to heal your own eyes?"

"Yes," Meir said. "I never knew your eyes had to be nurtured. I was encouraged to possess my own vision."

"You were sixteen at the time?"

"I had already gone through sixteen years of blindness," Meir said. "I was using a very high lens, 38 diopters, fitted for me by the ophthalmologist, in order to see a single letter. But it caused me massive headaches."

"What is your eye-chart rating now?"

"From three inches I can see print 20/20. That's not normal, but it is incredibly good for me. My vision from far is around 20/80. I was tested three times by the California Division of Motor Vehicles and now have a regular drivers license."

I remembered the introduction to Meir's book. It struck me as very controversial. So I decided to ask him about it.

"You begin your book saying 'No ailment is incurable and hope should never be given up.' Why do you say no ailment is incurable?"

"I have not proven it by any means," Meir replied. "But I think it's really interesting that the statement appears so bizarre to the world. People don't even take it as a possibility. That's one of the reasons for my saying it."

"I don't understand," I admitted.

"Look, in this world we have AIDS, cancer, heart attacks. We have all kinds of problems. When we believe ailments are inevitable, we do little about them. But I think if we learn the resources we have in our bodies, we could create a healing process. When we do that, we create a healing atmosphere. And that healing atmosphere would create a situation where there would be no more ailments. With time, the world may evolve to be free of disease.

"I cannot prove what I say," Meir added, "but I think for God's sake some people ought to think this way with me."

I decided to change the subject, but Meir wouldn't let me.

"Your book is inspiring because of the many stories of people who had so-called incurable illnesses---"

"And if I didn't believe in what I'm telling you now," Meir interrupted, "I could not have helped those people."

"I see."

"I know that I can't heal the world," Meir went on. "I don't have that power. But I am able to help people help themselves. I may be able to get people together to believe in the same thing, like my students and clients. And if ten percent of the world would work in that direction, we might change it.

"I have seen muscular dystrophy patients walk---not become Olympic runners---but be able to walk, which is something totally unbelievable. I've seen MS patients recovering or improving or changing the process of decay to a process of growth."

"How many people have you worked with?"

"More than three thousand."

"What's your success rate?"

"From those who stick with me, above 95 percent. For those who came and went and didn't stick to the therapy, I have more than 70-percent success."

"But it is not MY success," Meir quickly added. "It is the success people have with themselves. Still, it is phenomenal."

"What kind of problems do you work with?"

"Arthritis, vision problems, polio, muscular dystrophy, multiple sclerosis, strokes, back problems."

"How did you move from working with vision problems to working with all these other areas?" I asked.

"I wasn't given a method to cure only my eyes," Meir said. "I was given a new outlook on the body. If you move more, you are more alive. Move less, less alive. As I worked on my own eyes, I began to feel incredible fatigue in my spine. I did not before have back pain, no medical history of back trouble.

"I learned that the back fatigue was a result of strain my eyes were always under while resisting light. So I had to work on my own body."

"How did you do that work?"

"I moved. I breathed. I did a lot of stretching, but not like Yoga. It was more like trying to connect with the cells. I call it 'body meditation.' It created a contact between me and my body, me and my back, me and my legs."

Right here a young couple wandered over and interrupted our conversation.

"Excuse me," said the dark-haired woman. "We were overhearing your conversation and we want you to know you can only get your answers in the Bible."

Oh, brother. And they were looking right at me.

"This man is confused," she said, pointing at Meir. "You can't get help from him."

"Do you know he healed himself of blindness?" I asked.

"If he's healed, God did it. Not him. He's doing the devil's work by taking credit for the healing."

Meir rolled his eyes and sighed. I felt embarrassed.

"Listen, I am interviewing him. I am a writer."

They smiled. They were visibly glad to hear I wasn't sucked into Meir's "evil" world. The couple left right after I thanked them for their concern about me.

"I'm sorry, Meir," I said.

"I get that all the time."

"You do?" I was surprised. I hadn't thought about it before.

"People like to avoid responsibility. If you have an illness, work on it. You aren't powerless. God gave you the power to heal yourself. It isn't evil."

"Some people," I muttered. I took a deep breath and continued my conversation with Meir by asking a question that had been on my mind a long time. I was almost afraid to ask it.

"We're talking about self-healing and your book is called *Self-Healing*, but when people are sick, they come to you or another outside source. Why do you advise looking outside ourselves when you say the power is INSIDE ourselves?"

"We have not been educated to heal ourselves," Meir said without a pause. Obviously someone had asked him this question before. "The education we get says you have no power, you don't know anything. That's why you need somebody who has a good education in self-healing."

"Like you?"

"Like me, or maybe a tai chi instructor or someone trained in bodywork therapy. Some people simply read the Bates book and toss their glasses."

"My wife did that years ago," I shared. But Meir was on a roll. He wanted to keep talking. I let him.

"You have more chances for improvement with an instructor than just a book. He might have an insight to what you need."

"How do you work with people?"

"You come to me with a problem and I work with you. Then you go home and invent work for yourself. You come back to me and share what you invented and what you learned. We go back and forth until you eventually teach me more than what I know about you. I encourage you and support you."

"What about people who don't have the motivation to begin work on themselves?"

"There's nothing you can do about that," Meir said. "Nothing. The only thing I can do is influence those ten percent who are already motivated."

"Your teaching seems very intuitive and unstructured," I said. "Do you have any plan of treatment in mind when you meet someone?"

"I don't create the program in advance. I am trying to develop in other people the intuition to work on themselves. I want you to know your heart. I don't want you to know it twenty years from now when you have a heart attack. I want you to know it now and feel what it needs in this moment."

I was very impressed. I looked down at my list of questions to see if I had missed asking anything. I had.

"What are the elements of self-healing?"

"You have to believe you are worth the time and effort," Meir said. "Most people don't think that way. They have to provide for their family and so on. You should be responsible to your family, yes. But you are also responsible for your problems. You are not responsible for your disease but you are responsible TO it."

I walked Meir back to the terminal and saw that he got on the plane. It had been an amazing conversation. Thrilling and illuminating. And inspiring.

Two years later Meir and I met again. He was flying overseas and stopped in Houston to say hello. I was amazed at how well his eyes looked. He still blinked a lot. He still passed his hand over his eyes every few minutes. But he was clearly more advanced in his healing. His eyes had a controlled clarity to them. He didn't need me to read his ticket this time. Meir obviously takes his own advice and does the exercises he needs to keep himself growing.

We had a nice chat. This time we talked about the necessity for taking breaks at work, and for stretching, to keep our bodies alive and healthy. Whereas my first meeting with him became the cover story on the February '88 issue of *EAST WEST* magazine, I never wrote about the second meeting. (Not until now, anyway.)

I will never forget Meir. He is a fascinating man and a source of strength to me. When I want to do anything and I think it is impossible, I think of Meir. If he can heal himself of incurable blindness, if he can help thousands to see again, or to walk again, then what can I do in my own life?

As always, the only limits we have are the ones we believe in. Truth is, anything is possible.

And Meir is living proof of it.

Chapter Five

PSYCHIC GUERRILLA WAR GAMES
Stuart Wilde and the infamous WAM technique

I thought Stuart Wilde was strange. We were having breakfast and he was telling me about his new seminar, "The Quickening," in which he taught people how to play "psychic guerilla war games." It was a technique he used, he told me, to make people aware of their power. What do you do with the power once you get it? "That's up to you," Wilde said. "I'd take that power away if I told you how to use it."

Wilde had been around the world a half-dozen times. He had studied metaphysics in England, and he spoke about Eastern topics from direct experience. Though he could talk about everything from Tarot cards to channeling, Wilde wasn't gullible or insincere. He told me there are a lot of New Age scams out there, and he believed channeling was one of them.

"If your Uncle Frank was as thick as two planks when he was alive," Wilde explained, "he's no bloody smarter now that he's dead."

Wilde went on to tell me that you can't "channel" anything that isn't already in you. "It'd be like trying to get a piano to play a note that isn't in it. It ain't possible."

I had read Wilde's earlier books (**Miracles, The Force** and **Affirmations**) and liked them. I liked his humor and friendly style. But I found his talk about esoteric matters a bit wild (no pun intended). As we had breakfast and he told me about seeing the astral plane, I thought he was nuts. "The astral plane is a lot like this one," Wilde told me. "It isn't long robes and a lot of fog."

I couldn't argue with him. I hadn't seen the astral plane myself. So I listened quietly.

"And the tunnel that people talk about seeing when they have a near-death experience isn't really a tunnel. It's more like two energies that swirl into each other."

"I see," I said.

Wilde knew I was skeptical. No doubt my vibes were being read loud and clear by this British rogue. At one point, while I was cutting into my English muffin and buttering it, Wilde looked at me with the sweetest smile I had ever seen. I wondered if he was sending me some sort of astral command. I had heard he believed in thought control and mind reading.

"Why don't you come to my seminar?" he asked.

"Me?"

And the following Saturday I and about three hundred others (most of whom paid $85 for the day) discovered the awesome strength of a controlled thought.

PSYCHIC GUERRILLA WAR GAMES

The exercises Wilde led us through were called psychic guerilla war games. Wilde believes he was a Mongolian warrior long, long ago, and carries his fascination for that notorious clan into his seminars.

I paired off with Wendy, a charming woman who I felt very attracted to. Wilde told me to put up a force field around myself with my mind. "Just cover yourself with a white light---if you think THAT will work," he added with a sly grin, "or imagine a lead wall around you. Do whatever you want to protect yourself."

I conjured up a thick lead wall in my mind that NO ONE could possibly ever penetrate.

"Your partner is going to send a concentrated beam of energy into you, right through that wall of yours."

No way. I was not about to let this charming wench before me beat me at this esoteric mind game. My macho image needed to remain intact---no matter what. So I thickened the mental wall around me. And then I added a force field like the one Star Trek uses. No one was entering my space!

"Ready?" Wilde asked. "Go!"

I sat there with my eyes closed. All my attention was on this mental image of my wall of protection. For a few seconds I felt safe and comfortable. Even smug. But then I felt something---I'm not sure what to call it---push at my chest. I intensified my concentration on my lead wall and force field. The pressure in my chest got stronger. I felt a twisting energy forcing itself into me, like a laser cutting through cement. I panicked. My heart pounded, my breathing grew rapid and shallow. This couldn't be happening! This can't be a THOUGHT pushing into me!

But it was. My partner had put her focus on her beam of concentrated energy and she shot it into me. Right past by lead wall and force field. Thanks for nothing, Captain Kirk.

After the exercise Wilde asked for feedback. Everyone had experienced the power of the other's thought.

"Did the white light protect you?" Wilde asked.

"No!" everyone shouted.

"The white light of protection is a joke," Wilde said. "It ain't gonna protect you from nuttin'!"

Then we switched. My sexy partner put up her mental wall and I turned on my mental drill. In seconds I felt my thought enter her. I smiled to myself, content to know she so quickly weakened under the force of my mind.

"Isn't there any protection from someone's thoughts?" some concerned person asked Wilde. "If the white light doesn't protect us, what will?"

"I have good news and bad news about that," Wilde said. "The bad news is nuttin' can protect you from controlled thought. The good news is you don't need protection. You just need to be the one sending the thoughts. Most blokes don't use their minds. They are used BY them. I want you to come out of the mechanical world and claim your power."

There were more guerrilla war games. I became fascinated by the power of my mind. Though I had always read that our thoughts have power, Wilde gave us concrete experiences of that power. It was undeniable and unforgettable. I began to realize that if you could hold a thought in your mind long enough, with all the concentration and persistence of a warrior (not worrier), then you could make that thought influence reality. Mind-reading and thought-probing were indeed possible. Wilde was proving it.

WHAT DOES 'LITTLE YOU' WANT?

Later in the seminar Wilde led us through a remarkable imagery experience. We were asked to outline our own bodies in a ray of white light. "Use a finger or a beam," Wilde suggested. "Trace your body with the white light."

I found myself centering remarkably fast. I felt myself relax into the here and now. All tensions slipped out my body. I let go. I felt present like never before.

"Now make a beam of light from the top of your head to the floor in front of your feet."

I did. I could see it like a walkway for ants. For some reason I thought of the joke about two mental patients who want to escape their prison. One says he'll turn on the flash light and the other can walk out by walking on the ray of light. The other said, "You think I'm crazy? I'll get half way out, and you'll turn the light off!"

Wilde now urges us to create a mental image of ourselves and shrink it down. "Now have that image walk down the ray of light, from the top of your head to the floor," Wilde instructs. Oh God, I think. This IS a joke!

But I do what I'm told. Little Joe walks down my mental beam and gets to the floor. I watch in my mind as this midget image of me walks around my shoes and looks around the room.

"Just observe what your image does," Wilde says.

My little guy seems a bit confused. He decides he doesn't know where to go or what to do, so he just sits on the end of my shoe and watches Wilde with me.

After a few minutes Wilde has us bring the guy back up the light, grow to full size, and then merge with our bodies.

"What was that like for you?" Wilde asks everyone.

A tall man stands and says, "It was confusing. My miniature image didn't know what to do."

"Do YOU know what you want to do?" Wilde asked.

"Well, ah, I think so."

"Someone else?" Wilde asked.

"My shrunken me had fun. She ran around and looked for coins on the floor!"

"Great!" Wilde says. "Anyone else?"

I stand up.

"MY little one just sat on my shoe and did nothing," I say.

"Why nothing?" Wilde asks.

"I guess he wanted to know WHAT to do."

"Are you caught up in right and wrong, Joe?" Wilde asks me. "If your image didn't know what to do, maybe he was afraid to make a move unless he knew what the right move would be. Is that how you live your life?"

"I dunno," I say.

"Think about it," Wilde says. "Anyone else?"

Turns out that this little imagery technique was remarkably revealing. Whatever the little person did at the end of the beam---or didn't do---revealed something about how we act in our day-to-day lives. Fascinating. Everyone learned something about themselves from this unique experience.

ASTRAL SEX

The final psychic guerrilla war game of the day involved all of us lying on the floor and getting comfortable. Again we outlined our bodies with a pin-pointed ray of light. But this time Wilde had us LEAVE our bodies.

"Just get up out of your body," Wilde said. "See your astral self slide out of your physical body."

It was easy! I actually felt an essence within me rise from my prone body. How was this possible? I can't tell you for certain. It seemed to occur due to my intense concentration and as a result of the day's experiences. Everything we had done led to this grand moment.

"Turn your astral body around," Wilde said. "Do a few flips in the air."

About then I noticed my female partner's astral body. Even it was attractive. I found my astral body drifting over to her astral body. Wilde's voice dwindled in importance as I got nearer to my partner. A warrior wouldn't worry about doing the right thing here, I told myself. Go for it!

I let my astral self unite with my partner's astral self. It was very nice. No, it didn't have the same feel as a physical connection. There wasn't any real FEEL at all, actually. But we could sense each other and somehow it was very sensuous. I'll never forget it.

Wilde brought us all back into our bodies. As I stretched and looked around the room, I saw my partner stretching and looking around the room. I didn't know if I should make eye contact or what, but since I was becoming a warrior, I faced my fears and looked right at her. She smiled and winked!

The day ended after that. I never did see my partner again but I've tried to find her through the astral circuit. So far I haven't had much luck.

WARRIOR'S WISDOM

I still hear from Stuart Wilde, however. He is now doing a five-day intensive called "Warrior's Wisdom" in the mountains of Taos, New Mexico. In this fear-inducing seminar, Wilde has people walk on hot coals, climb shaking poles, leap off mountain edges, and wrestle with wild animals. That's what I'm told, anyway. I haven't personally done the seminar---yet! (I'm waiting for Wilde to invite me to it as his guest. And I don't mind waiting.)

Why does Wilde have people do all these death-defying (I assume people defy death there) things?

"People feel alive when they are challenged," Wilde told me. "My father said the best time of his life was when he was being shot at while rescuing people in war. Most people want more excitement in their lives than just working with computers all day. I give "em somethin to talk about."

That he does!

Wilde sent me his latest book recently. It's called ***The Trick to Money is Having Some!*** I don't like the title but I love the book. Wilde is a practical metaphysician. "If you can't take a philosophy to the bank," he once told me, "it's frickin' worthless!"

We live in the material world and our real test is how well we do in it. Most New Agers think money is bad. Not Stuart Wilde. "Money is a game you play with YOURSELF!" Wilde says.

One of the most wonderful things I got from Wilde's money book is the concept of WAM. "WAM" could very well become the mantra for the metaphysical movement. WAM is something we should say morning, noon, and night. Whenever you enter a negotiation, say WAM to yourself. Whenever someone asks you for something, remember WAM. We might even consider creating a new God called WAM.

What is WAM? WAM is a mantra meaning "What About Me?"

At first it may seem like a self-indulgent reminder to be egotistic and greedy. Actually, it is more a reminder to respect yourself.

Chapter Six

THE HOTTEST SEMINAR AROUND: FIREWALKING

All we know is still infinitely less

than all that still remains unknown.

-- William Harvey

I can still see the bed of glowing coals. It was six feet long, four feet wide. And hot. REAL hot. I stood at the edge of the bed, in a circle with some twenty other seekers, and felt the heat pushing against my chest. It was undeniably real.

You've been near an outdoor grill after the coals have burned down to a red glaze. You've felt the heat. You've watched ground meat patties sizzle and brown into hamburgers and hot dogs get those black stripes from the hot grill. You knew better than to touch the coals. You always wore big mittens. You were careful when you turned the burgers or dogs over so you wouldn't get burned.

Magnify that grill. Turn it into a bed of coals on the ground. Red HOT coals you are standing near and preparing to walk on. Can you imagine that? I can. I was there. I looked at those coals and felt their heat and thought what IN THE WORLD was I doing here? Why in all hell was I not only thinking about walking across those molten nuggets, I was about to do it???

WHY??!!

WHY WALK WHEN YOU CAN RUN?

You don't sign up to do a firewalk and just walk across the coals. There is a four-hour seminar right before the actual walk. In that seminar you are taught "how" to walk on the coals. But that's really not true. No one knows why you can walk---or cannot---walk on fire. Some people get burned. Some don't. Michael Sky, a popular firewalking seminar leader, says if you walk on fire five or more times, you are bound to get what he calls an "ouchie."

So why walk? And why pretend anyone can teach you how to safely do it?

I wanted to walk on coals because it was the hottest seminar experience going around. I figured if I could walk on fire, I could do anything. Later I learned you don't really walk on fire. You walk on coals. I also learned that in a city as big as Houston, there weren't any firewalkers. Enterprising fellow that I am, I decided to bring one in.

Ed Richards is a piano tuner out of Chicago. He learned firewalking from the movement's founder, Tolly Burkan. I don't suppose Richards would be known for anything if it weren't for the firewalk. Same goes for Tolly. The hot bed brings a lot of media attention to otherwise mediocre teachers. Still, Ed seemed like a nice enough guy to me. I trusted him.

But I couldn't pull it off. Dealing with fire codes and trying to convince 15 people that firewalking was THE thing to do for self-growth wasn't easy (even though thousands have done the firewalk). I tried. But I soon gave up. And I gave up when I learned of Richard Hite, a firewalking instructor, trained by Peggy Burkan (Tolly's ex), who lived right here in Houston.

RICHARD HITE: THE MAN WITH THE KEYES

Richard Hite has over twenty years of metaphysical and spiritual experience under his belt. He also has more than one belt. He has three black belts in several styles of martial arts, including Karate and Tae Kwon Do. Richard is a hypnotherapist, breath worker, Yoga instructor, speaker, artist, psychotherapist, transpersonal counselor, and one of a handful of authorized firewalking instructors.

"What I help people do is overcome the trauma of dealing with life," explains Hite, who looks like a large version of singer James Taylor. While working at psychiatric hospitals Hite specialized in recovery from post-traumatic stress syndrome. But he believes each of us is working on a recovery of one sort or another.

"We are addicted to being alive and we are addicted to avoiding life," Richard, 37, explains. "What I do is help you recover your inner divinity, your essential Self, the Self that is hidden under your fears and traumas. That deeper Self is pure love."

Hite uses a variety of tools to help clients and workshop participants free themselves from their self-imposed prisons. Like a great magician, he will use whatever is available to help you awaken from your dream. His magic tricks include hypnosis, NLP (neural-linguistic programming), meditative music, Tibetan gongs, guided writing, and breath work.

"The breath work may be the most powerful of all the available tools," says Hite. He initially learned the breathing process from a Tibetan Yoga teacher. Hite has since integrated that teacher's method with the breath work developed by Wilhelm Reich, Otto Rank, Stan Grof, and Austin therapist Jacquie Small. Hite has also created new methods, including using a gong to feel deeper vibrations in the body while breathing. Hite's original breath work techniques are, he says, cleansing and get immediate results.

"Let me give you an example," he says. "In Mirror Breathing you sit in front of a mirror with a partner. You watch yourself in the mirror as you breathe deep and long, way down into your diagram. Your partner watches your face and body to see if you begin to show signs of tension or resistance. When they notice a change, they point it out to you. The result is an extremely intense form of breathing that unlocks cellular memory and opens the doors for stuck energies to begin to move again. You may cry, laugh, shake, remember old events that shaped your life, or any number of things."

"Mirror Breathing is powerful," Hite adds. He invented the process to help people accept themselves. "Mirror Breathing helps you experience profound self-acceptance while releasing negative emotions."

Breathing is great, but the firewalking seminar is still THE potent tool in Hite's bag of transformation tricks.

"The fire brings you into the now," Hite said. "It is a modern rite of passage that transforms your relationship to fear."

He holds up a large color photograph of himself standing on a bed of red-hot coals while also holding burning coals in his hands. Neither his hands nor feet were burned, he says.

"Anything is possible if you stick with your intention despite your fears," he explained. "The trick is to learn not to mind that you have fear. What you want to do is transform the fear into personal power through a loving relationship with your higher self."

Richard is also fond of asking questions and telling stories. Similar to the manner of famous hypnotherapist Milton Erickson, Richard will look at a client, smile, and ask, "How good can you stand your life?" or "How much are you willing to accept right now?"

"Too many of us are afraid to accept goodness," Hite explains. "You believe you don't deserve it and you push it away. Well, just how good can you stand it? The universe is bestowing gifts on us all the time. Are you accepting them?"

Richard's number one client has always been himself. He says he has worked on himself ever since he was a teenager in Missouri and realized that he had been a victim of multiple forms of abuse throughout his childhood.

"It's not an accident that today a lot of my clients are dealing with abuse issues," Richard said. "I can identify with them very easily. I had the same story to work on."

Richard has taken his twenty years of experience in personal growth, and his education (he has a BA in Education and an MA in Psychology) and developed a new system for healing and self-awareness called "The K.E.Y.E.S. Program."

"This program is an on-going group event that combines the best of what I know with universal principles and psycho-therapeutic techniques," Hite explained.

"The program moves you from where you are into new terrain. It moves you so fast and completely that you can't predict what you will be at the end because your prediction will come from who you are now. And that will change!"

Richard said the K.E.Y.E.S. Program is a safe, integrated, precise way to gain empowerment, self- actualization, peak performance and transpersonal awareness.

"The word K.E.Y.E.S. is an acronym," Hite explained. "The K stands for knowledge as well as "ki", or life energy. The E stands for enlightenment. The Y means Yoga or union with all life. The next E refers to empowerment as well as ecstasy. And the S stands for spirit or Self, the divine core of your life."

People have taken Hite's program (which lasts 12 weeks) and stopped smoking, healed headaches, TMJ, back pains, chest pains, PMS, and arthritis. They have also recovered from trauma, broken through fear and anger, and found new, more powerful ways to be alive. Many have ended destructive relationships and begun new, more loving ones.

"All I do is help you uncover and trust your own inner expertise," Hite said. "I just guide you through your feelings and into your healings. You do all the work, not me. What I teach you is to have a therapeutic relationship with your divine self. The firewalk is one place where I do this in a powerful and unforgettable way."

Hite invited me to his next walk. He sensed that I was committed to doing the walk and said I could come for free. He wasn't in this for the money, he told me. I later learned he didn't know how to handle money. "Give me a business and I'll run it into the ground," he told me. It was easier for him to just let people come to firewalks for free. It was an offer I couldn't refuse. But I wanted to.

Fear arose in me like you wouldn't believe. I wanted to get sick or have an emergency. I wanted to avoid the walk. I wondered why I was doing this. What was I going to get out of it? Why walk on FIRE, for God's sake? Couldn't I do something simple like read a book? Or maybe see a film and have a test?

Right there is the whole point of the firewalk. It brings up fear so you learn to be comfortable with it. There's a book out called *Feel The Fear And Do It Anyway*. I felt fear standing in front of those coals. But I knew I'd walk anyway. So firewalking is a profound way to transform your relationship with fear. I've heard that a brave person is a coward who acted anyway. I was brave the night I walked on hot coals. Shaking inside, wanting to run from the hotbed before me, I chose to walk anyway.

I got burned, of course. But that's a later part of this story.

FOR SALE: FOUR HOURS

How do you walk on fire?

"One step at a time," Hite told me.

There's no secret to firewalking. The purpose is for you to feel fear and yet act anyway. But many firewalkers are using the walk to sell their beliefs. And that's where I think people get misguided and misinformed.

Tolly Burkan was a magician and a circus performer. His seminar has magic tricks and talks about illusion. He says fear is "False Evidence Appearing Real" or FEAR. He also talks about creating your own reality. Yet Tolly was in a car accident and had difficulty recovering. You wonder why he created THAT for himself.

Tony Robbins, probably the best-known firewalker, allegedly stole the firewalking seminar from Burkan and created some stories about how he learned it from an Indian guru. Robbins uses the walk to sell NLP, a high-tech but confusing way to pay close attention to how people communicate so you can make them, supposedly, do your bidding.

Richard Hite is more spiritual. He uses the walk to sell inner guidance and love. I recall him saying in the seminar that love was what helped you get across the fire. He used to be a karate instructor and said once, in a locker room, his hand automatically flew up in the air. It "coincidentally" blocked a punch a youth was trying to deliver. "That was love," Richard said. It was? Seems to me it was more like a sharp reflex from a man trained to respond in exactly that way. But no one else questioned what Hite was selling.

Scientists use the walk to sell their beliefs in science. I remember seeing a scientist on Johnny Carson one night. He was there to prove firewalking was a trick. He made his own bed of coals and walked on it. Because he made it across okay, he said firewalking was a joke. So he used the walk to sell his own belief in the natural law that keeps your feet moist so you don't get burned.

What REALLY happens in the walk?

INSIDE OUT

Since anything can be said in the seminar preceding the walk, the seminar doesn't matter. One fellow at my walk never heard a single word of Hite's seminar. Yet this man walked without harm. I can easily imagine a seminar where a leader tells a group that "You WILL get burned!" and then that group will walk and some will get burned, some won't.

The fire is the fire. Period. What you say about it reveals more about you than anything else. When Robbins raves about NLP at the walk, it says he loves NLP. When Hite talks of inner direction, it reveals what he believes. When the scientist says natural law explains it all, he reveals his heart-felt belief. The fire becomes a mirror revealing the true you. You can't lie to the fire. It is the ultimate test of truth.

I stood in front of the coals and knew I was going to walk next. But I felt the heat from the glowing bed and took two steps back. I swallowed. I looked at that l-o-n-g bed of coals and thought of running. I gulped some air, told myself to just do it, and began to walk with determined steps.

The first step felt like walking on gravel. The second step felt like walking on broken rocks on a warm beach. Right then I told myself I ought to be burned and, sure enough, I felt a blister on my foot. I screamed NO to myself and walked the rest of the way across without injury.

A fellow on the other side of the hotbed turned a water hose on my feet to wash away any lingering coals. I could feel the blister. My feet felt hot. Achy. But not damaged. And I knew that the blister I got was a reminder that my thoughts influenced what I experienced. I thought I should get a blister and behold! I got one!

Some people got blisters, some didn't. One person fell to the ground before the walk and cried like a baby. He was too scared to walk. We all went to him and held him, letting him know it was okay to walk, or not to walk. When we settled into going back to the seminar room, this same man knelt and washed our feet. He didn't wash mine, but seeing him do this made me feel powerful. It made him look holy.

Most of the people who walked were high. Ecstatic even. They were so happy, so excited, so up, because they had done it. They felt fear and walked nonetheless. I seemed to be the only person who thought it was no big deal. Okay, so I walked on fire. What's next?

I was disappointed for several days. The blister on my foot reminded me that I create my experience, so I looked at everyday events differently, wondering how I created them. I met with Hite a few days afterward for lunch. I told him the seminar part of the event didn't do much for me. It seemed to be a hodgepodge, crockpot selection of information which may or may not apply to anything. He said, "You didn't need the seminar; you needed the fire."

Good answer. The fire brought me into the now, the point of power in every situation. And the fire taught me to feel the fear and do it anyway. To act despite the feelings I have. And for that, I am grateful. I now have a better relationship with fear. I've been asked to play the harmonica in front of people. Fear comes up for me when I consider doing that. But I know I can handle it. If I can walk on a bed of hot coals, I can toot my harp for an audience. And I know my audience will never give me a blister.

TWO YEARS LATER

It's been close to two years since I did the walk. I had lunch yesterday with Hite. I asked him, "What is the purpose of the seminar? It seems like you can use those four hours to say anything you feel like."

"The purpose is to have people feel fear over and over again in a variety of ways."

"Why?"

"So they are comfortable with it. So they learn not to mind it."

Again, the firewalk is a modern rite of passage, a type of Yuppie obstacle course, that teaches you how to feel the fear but act anyway. Maybe Michael Sky, in his wonderful book on firewalking, said it best. He said if you have a clear intention and a strong belief and a supportive environment, you can increase your odds of success. The firewalk is a place where you intend to walk, you learn to believe you can do it, and the environment is one where you are encouraged to do it. But whether you get burned or not is unpredictable.

"Good thing," Sky says. "If the firewalk wasn't dangerous, there would be no point in doing it."

Ah, yes. Feel the fear and do it anyway. It's a primary rule for success in life, as well as in the firewalk. No, I don't intend to do the firewalk again. Once is enough for me.

When it comes to walking barefoot across a bed of hot coals, once is enough for anybody.

Chapter Seven

THE FORUM

Zen-ized Family Therapy

or,

Freeing The Past To Create The Future

You can have all the fairies you like in your back garden,

just as long as you know that you put them there.

-- Ray Woollam, *On Choosing - With A Quiet Mind*

I can leave if I want. Here's my chance. It's the beginning of two weekends in Werner Erhard's Forum. Ed Gerowitz, this weekend's leader, is inviting us to split with a full refund of our $600. "If you've been pressured to be here," Ed says, "leave now." I feel pressure all right, but it's internal. No one threatened me or forced me to come. Only one person out of the 105 here today takes the offer.

And the Forum begins. Over the next two entire weekends, from 9 a.m. to after midnight each day, I will experience unbearable fear, headaches so fierce they threaten to crack my skull, disappointment, rage, tears, laughter, insight, and a nearly irresistible urge to walk out. Had I known all this on the morning of the first day, I just might have taken Ed up on his offer.

FROM est TO THIS

In the beginning was "est", short for Erhard's Seminar Training. Werner Erhard, originally called Jack Rosenberg, was an former car salesman and serious seeker of truth who had an unusual experience while driving on a California freeway. At that time no one knew what Werner went through. Today we might say he had a moment of enlightenment, when he somehow understood (or maybe accepted) the way of the world. Werner then created a new seminar program called est.

est was a two-weekend, hard-hitting, controversial experience called everything from Western Zen to brainwashing. It was known for its militaristic approach and strict rules (no breaks, no food, no talking, no leaving the room). Anyone who took the course "got" something out of it, because whatever they got was, as they say in Werner's circle, what they got. Despite these apparently negative characteristics, est attracted more than 500,000 people in twelve years. In 1984 Werner retired est and in its place began to offer the Forum, a much milder yet just as effective new intensive seminar.

WEEKEND ONE: THE MOST DANGEROUS PERSON

Ed Gerowitz, a former child psychologist, somehow reminds me of my father. Maybe it's his big nose. Maybe, too, it's the fact that the Forum pulls up a lot of family history and each of us projects our father onto the Forum leader, whoever he might be. I don't know. A few said Ed looked and acted like a drill sergeant (my father had been a Marine sergeant). All agreed he was powerful, loud, forceful and direct. We liked him.

We're told the ground rules for the Forum. You go to the bathroom whenever there is a break (once every three hours). You are not to eat on the breaks except at the designated meal break (abut 7:30 p.m.). You are also asked to promise not to drink alcohol during the Forum (including the week between the weekends) and not to take any medicine (unless prescribed by your doctor). In addition, you are asked not to talk between breaks unless you are called on, and then you are to stand and wait for a Forum assistant to bring a microphone to you. None of these "rules" are something we "have" to do, but we are asked to promise to keep the rules. We're told that if we leave the room for even two minutes, "you may get the result, but you have no right to expect the result." No one knows what "the result" is, however.

One woman asks Ed why she can't take notes during the Forum (another rule).

"Did I tell you that you can't take notes?" Ed asks. But it's a rhetorical question. "We ask you to promise not to take notes; we don't say you can't take them." Few of us see the point. But it's no big deal. None of us really want to take notes, anyway.

The rules and our promise to keep them take more than two hours to cover. Why? My guess is that we are being shown how irresponsible we are. Normally we say we will do something, don't do it, and then think up an excuse to justify the behavior. Ed wants us to see how we "slime out" of our agreements with ourselves and others. I can't help thinking about a friend of mine who is a felon when it comes to responsibility. He'd get a lot out of this segment of the Forum, I think. As for me, I'm getting a headache and feeling bored silly.

Ed talks about boredom. It's a "clearing" (a what?) that I bring to the situation. Each of us has a clearing of some nature which paints every scene. It's like looking through foggy glasses and saying the world is foggy. It's the glasses, not the world. Some of us have clearings that say our parents are never satisfied with what we do. One woman stands, takes the mike, and says her father is never pleased with her, even though she is a successful businesswoman (most of the attendees are successful in terms of the world).

"You're a jerk!" Ed declares. We're surprised to hear this. It's more confrontational than we expected. I'm nervous now, but also excited, as if I were watching a dramatic movie happen right before my eyes.

"My father isn't happy with me," the woman says. I'm surprised she's standing her ground, not moving or shaking or crying (as I might have done).

"You're a jerk!" Ed repeats. "Your father is so proud of you he can't stand it. He may not know how to say it, that's all."

"You don't know my father," the woman counters.

"You people are so damned blind," Ed says in that always-too-loud voice. "All your parents every wanted for you was for you to be happy!"

Chills go up my spine. My eyes get moist with tears. Ed's comment has hit me right between the eyes. I haven't seen my family in nine years. Though they are only a plane ride away, I have refused to go home. My bitterness over the past, my refusal to forgive, has kept me at bay. And now I feel like a jerk. I start to cry. So does the woman standing.

"You know what you do to your parents?" Ed asks. "You hold your happiness from them. They want you to be happy and you're all such jerks you don't ever tell them what they most want to hear!"

And so it goes. Ed tells us we are here to explore what it means "to be a being." He spends a lot of time describing the difference between reality and our interpretations of reality. We learn that we "story" everything we experience, and that we don't experience the experience. Most of us are thinking more deeply than ever before. And most of us are getting unforgettable headaches. People take turns sharing the dark secrets of their lives while Ed listens and comments. Somehow sharing and hearing everyone else share brings a peace.

When we break into groups of four, we're asked to answer a Zen-like question: "Where in your life have you thingified your life?" I hate the absurdity of the coined word and the illogic of the question. But I soon recognize it as a westernized koan (unanswerable question) designed to break up the patterns of my mind.

Later we are given an equally distressing question: "Where in your life have you turned beauty into the floor?" Despite the absurdity of the questions, we can answer them in ways that are insightful. One woman learns she "thingified" her relationship with her husband so it was no longer alive. I discover how beauty is in each person but I often look at it as I do the floor, blind to its reality.

On the evening of the first day Ed asks us to "pick a troublesome problem to work on, something that won't go away which, if it did leave, would make a vast difference in your life." Ed wants more than a label, however. "Fear" isn't good enough. He wants to know what the bodily sensations are that accompany fear. By now I have a headache that threatens to kill me. I also want to escape. My legs are actually twitching with desire to run out of the room. I don't know what I am about to face, but I don't want to face it. The only reason I stay seated is because I promised to stay seated.

Ed leads us through the "truth exercise," as he calls it, where you focus on the problem you have picked. Since my headache is overwhelming, I focus on it. Ed asks questions which keep us focused on our physical being. It hurts. My mind wants to think of something pleasant. But I stick with the pain. It's excruciating. I want to die and get this over with. Ed keeps talking, keeps directing our attention to the sensations. Fifteen minutes later he stops. I notice my headache is still there, but very tolerable. I'm more relaxed. I'll live.

"You're used to escaping from your problems," Ed tells us. "Focus on them and you can disappear them." Again, we don't really understand. But it's late, we're tired, and we're dismissed.

Sunday is more of the same. But Ed suddenly starts talking about other seminar programs available through Werner Erhard and Associates. Most of us find this blatant advertising a waste of our time. But as Ed continues sharing his personal experiences in some of the other programs, I begin to understand how powerful they can be. The other seminars are nearly all once a week for ten weeks, and for the reasonable price of about $80 each. They are essentially support groups to help you stay with your progress and your promises to create changes in your life. Still, Ed spends two hours discussing these other programs, and most of us would rather be having dinner.

The most powerful exercise of the first weekend occurs late Sunday night. We pair off and Ed tells us to stare into each other's eyes. "Notice the fear," he says. I don't. "If you don't feel fear, imagine that everybody in this room is out to kill you." I'm feeling fear now. "Imagine everyone in Houston wants to hurt you," Ed continues. Fear has my guts twisted. My partner's eyes are wide as she feels fear, too. Ed keeps us in fear for far longer than I think is healthy. Then he switches.

"Imagine you are the most dangerous man," Ed says. "Your partner is afraid of you." I feel more comfortable with this. "Now imagine everyone in the room is afraid of you, and then everyone in Houston." Energy pumps through me as I realize I have the power to do whatever I want, without fear of others.

Everyone in the room seems more alive now. We're all dangerous. That doesn't mean we're going to hurt people. It simply means we are empowered. We have no one to fear.

Shortly afterwards we're dismissed with a reminder to keep our promises throughout the week. I still have a headache and I'm still confused. Ed told us we ought to be feeling shaken up. We do. I tell my wife that I feel like a goldfish in a bowl of water. Like most goldfish, I've never been out of my "clearing." The Forum is like another fish dropping in on me and saying, "How do you like the water?" I say, "What water?" The fish says, "Have you ever been out?" "Out?" I ask. "Out of what?!"

WEEKEND TWO: THE MEANING OF THE SCAR

Roger Armstrong is an ex-minister and former company executive, originally from Houston. He's this weekend's Forum leader, and most of us want Ed back. Roger is less direct, not quite as articulate, and somehow softer. Maybe it's the fact that he is bald and somewhat overweight. We begin this weekend with a discussion about comparison and how it stops us from experiencing the reality of this moment.

After that, Roger points out that two people from our group haven't shown up today. He wants to know if we care about that. Most of us don't. I don't even know who those two people are. We're reminded of our promises and asked to stand if we violated any of them. Nearly everyone gets on their feet. "You see," Roger says, "you support each other in not supporting each other." We sit down, ashamed.

Roger talks about our past and says we're going to do intense work. We're going to find out what makes us "the being that we are." "If you're not up for this," he tells us, "leave now. We'll give you all your money back if you go right now." No one leaves.

Throughout the day we are told to consider what our "conversation" is. A conversation is like Ed's clearing; it's our programming, our way of being, what makes "me" me. It's another Zen-like device to get us to step out of ourselves. I notice that I am a conversation for control. Roger asks me to say, "I am that I am a conversation for control." I obey but feel pretty dumb. Others are conversations for victims, for being right, for dependency.

People share their stories and we all, in some form or other, learn something about ourselves through them. One woman was a child prostitute. Her father was her pimp. She ran away from him when she was 16. Now, twenty years later, she is ready to forgive him. Her story moves us all. I think to myself, if she can forgive her father for the crimes against her, why can't I forgive mine for his simple injustices?

One man stands and says he just realized that his parents made a tremendous sacrifice for him when he was 16. He had "done something awful" when he was a teenager and his family uprooted and moved to protect him. What did he do? Did he kill somebody? Roger encouraged the man to open up, to dump the secret pain. "I was caught playing doctor," the man said. Obviously it was a big deal to him. But now, after sharing his story, he felt free to call his parents and thank them for their love and support. It was a monumental moment in his life. Again we were all touched. Our secret pains hurt more because they are secret rather than because they are so wrong. Sharing the secrets frees us.

Roger says we carry the past around and we re-create it all the time. Women marry men like their father, men marry women like Mom. People who get divorced several times keep marrying the same type of person. We are slaves to our past.

Later we're asked to remember times in our life when we felt physical pain. "When did your bones get broken or your skin damaged?" Roger asks. This is extremely uncomfortable to consider. People recall hurts from long ago. One woman says she was hit in the head with a milking stool (her father was a farmer) when she was four years old. "Good," Roger says.

I remember being told about the scar on my left arm. I got it when I was about one year old. I put my arm in a milk bottle and then broke the bottle. But I didn't consciously recall anything. "It doesn't matter if you can't remember the experience," Roger reminds us. "If you felt pain and blacked out, your conversation used it to make decisions about your life."

Then we're asked to recall times when we felt shock or loss. Many people had friends who died of suicide. I easily recall the first dead person I ever saw, my grandmother, when I was about ten. I can feel the shock and confusion of that experience right now.

Roger helps us explore those past hurts in a way designed to help us be free of them. We separate into groups of four and speculate about our past incidents and what they could mean. I am amazed to discover that the scar on my arm suddenly has significance. When it happened, my parents called the family doctor. The doctor came to the house (those were the days) to look at my cut. My mother hid in a back room. My father held me while the doctor sewed up the cut. And I didn't cry (so my parents told me). What did it mean? Whenever I talk about my family I seldom mention my mother---as if she were out of the room! Whenever I speak of my father, it's with a feeling of pain. Understanding the scar helped me begin to see my parents in a clear way.

On Sunday Roger spends many hours (yes, hours) talking about the other seminars available. Here we go again, I think. One man stands, takes the mike, and says this commercializing is a waste of time. Roger stands toe to toe with this fellow and screams at all of us: "You people are so damned righteous! You allow million-dollar ad campaigns to sell you drugs and booze and cigarettes, stuff that kills you and your loved ones, and you complain about an $80 seminar that heals your life!"

The truth of what he said hit hard. I felt like collapsing right then and there. Roger was right. We complain about the Forum's advertising while we permit the destruction of the world. Obviously our thinking is screwed up. I felt differently about the promotional aspects of the Forum from then on.

113

Late Sunday Roger delivers the message of the Forum, one that is tough to get across on paper. "You're all machines," he said. "You have no choice but to do what you do. You're no better than robots." And he added an even more melancholy note: "Nothing matters in life. Nothing at all."

A couple of people stand and argue, but it's clear we're machines and we have no freedom. Even the people standing and debating with Roger are doing so because of their programming.

I'm depressed. And discouraged. Not because nothing matters and I'm a robot, but because I've heard this message before. I went through 60 hours of intense work, gave up two weekends and $600, got headaches that crippled me---all for something I already know!

When we broke into small groups I shared my unhappiness. Everyone else was silent and confused. "If nothing matters," one of my group members said, "what do you do?" "You do whatever you want," I said. "You're free." She heard me and understood. "I should have given you the $600," she said.

Back in our regular seats Roger explains the difference between an enlightened person vs. a non-enlightened one.

"Normally you get up in the morning, get dressed, go to work, and do your thing," he said. "But now that you are enlightened you will get up in the morning, get dressed, go to work, and do your thing."

He also said that now that we know what our conversation is, and now that we know we have no choice because of our programming, we are actually free to choose our future. It's like stepping out of the machine (or the goldfish bowl) and looking back. Now we know we have a choice.

Most of the rest of the day is about the other seminars and the power of our word. "Take a stand for something and you'll make it so," Roger says. "That's what John F. Kennedy did when he said we'd put a man on the moon. He made a promise to do something that was unreasonable when he said it. But he made it happen."

GRADUATION: YOUR NEXT SEMINAR

On Tuesday evening I and the other hundred or so Forum participants show up with a hundred guests. While we "graduate" from the Forum, our guests are taken to a few smaller rooms and invited to sign up for the next one.

Graduation consists of strong encouragement to do other seminars. We also do an exercise where we talk to another person while pretending we are speaking to our mother, or father, or other loved ones. Most of us need tissues for this. We also watch an old movie called "I Used To Be Different But Now I'm The Same", about Erhard's six-day workshop in California. We're also told that whenever we experience a breakdown in life, just focus on our original commitment and do something that honors it. If my promise is to get to a client and my car breaks down, my next action should be something that still gets me to my client.

At evening's end I am surprised to learn my wife has registered for the next Forum. It was a small miracle that she came to the introductory talk. I am staggered to discover she will do the next Forum. She apparently heard or saw something that intrigued her. Two days later she told me that two friends from work will do the Forum with her!

NOT THAT

What is it about the Forum that attracts so many people? The Erhard folks don't advertise. Everybody comes at the invitation of a friend. And the Forum doesn't pretend to be therapeutic. What they promise is a "breakthrough in personal effectiveness."

I find the Forum powerful and yet mysterious. It is part therapy, part Zen, part fly-by-the-seat-of-the-Forum-leader's-pants, and largely unique. The Forum seems to clean up the past so we can be totally in the present. And out of the power of the present we can create the future we want.

What is the Forum? Ultimately, I don't know. In the movie we watched on Tuesday, the seminar trainer for the six-day said the slogan for that experience could be "Not that." You can't describe the six-day, he said, because whatever you said was "not that." Whatever we said about the seminar would be our description of it, and not it.

Whatever we say about the Forum is also "not that."

AFTERTHOUGHTS

I did the Forum a year ago. What do I think about it now? I'm glad I did it but I wouldn't do it again. And I'm not so sure I'd recommend it to you or anyone else.

First, there is a certain randomness in the way the seminar is conducted. What you get out of the 60-odd hours is unpredictable. I remember Ed Gerowitz saying, "I take one aspirin every other day." Now why tell us THAT? It's an example of the sort of rambling that goes on in the Forum that may or may not be of value to you. For me, the seminar is too much like shooting an arrow in a dark room at an unknown target. Sure, you'll hit something. That arrow has to land SOMEplace. But will it be worth $600 and all the time spent? Who knows?

Second, there is far too much selling in the program. Well over 60% of the Forum is used to sell other Erhard seminars. Obviously Erhard is into self-preservation. He wants you to keep coming back. On one level this is worthwhile because it is a practical way to spend your money (better than buying more cigarettes, for example). But on another level, it's a major waste. If Erhard wanted to, he could give you the contents of ALL his courses in the Forum. But that would be too easy. And not very profitable.

Third, the Forum feels like surgery with a rusty knife. It'll help you relieve some pain, but the operation might hurt worse than the pain did. What I got from the Forum was a tremendous focus on results. They want you to ACT. To DO. To ACCOMPLISH. And if you have excuses or complaints, they say "JUST DO IT!" There is no room for love or acceptance. Or rather what they give you is a form of "tough love," where they are authoritative in order to get you to do something in your own best interest. But I find this type of healing primitive. What I've noticed about people who take the Forum and become Erhard junkies is that they become hard. There is a certain aloofness about them. As if they are all business and no heart. That, to me, is sad.

The Forum IS valuable for discovering what we all have in common. The sharing aspect of the seminar lets you know we are all very much alike. And the program does help you let go of the past so you can focus on the present. But how the seminar is presented isn't, to me, very wise. It's too confusing, rambling, and time-consuming.

That's my opinion, anyway. You can go to a free intro to the Forum in just about any major city in the U.S. But be prepared for a snow job. Erhard's people are trained salespeople. And they believe in their product. If you go, be prepared to either agree to do the Forum or to say a strong, unwavering NO! Anything in between will leave you open for a sales pitch.

Chapter Eight

YOUR BODY SPEAKS ITS MIND

"Where is your mind?"

S ometimes I begin one of my longer writing classes with that question. I get all sorts of answers. At first my students just look at me and wonder what I'm up to. "Isn't it obvious," they seem to be thinking, "that your mind is in your HEAD?"

Is it obvious? What do YOU think? Where is YOUR mind?

Since most of our senses are located in our head, or registered in our head, we tend to think our mind is right up there, too. Your eyes are there, your nose, mouth, ears. And when you feel something with your hands, it computes up there in your brain. So is that where your mind is?

Someone in my class usually states the obvious, "Your mind is in your brain."

"Is it?" I ask.

No doubt someone will say, "No, your mind is in your heart area."

"What do you mean?" I ask.

"Well," this person begins to explain, "Zen masters say they think from their *hara*, or stomach region. So maybe the mind is there."

"Bull!" someone else says. "That's nonsense. My mind isn't in MY stomach!"

If the class is big enough, someone else will sure enough add, "Your mind is wherever you put it."

"You can put your attention anywhere," I clarify. "But where is your mind physically located in your body?"

"Gotta be your brain," someone, usually an older man, declares. "Gotta be!"

"Everyone agree?" I ask.

Nope. If there are any teenagers present, they'll really spice up the dialogue. For some reason they are more open-minded and aware. I love them. One recently said, "Your mind can be part of a larger mind, like a big universal mind, and that means your mind isn't in your body at all."

"Mother Earth is one big Mama," another teenager might state. "We are just her cells. She is the mind, not us."

"Oh, Jeez," the older people in the class grumble.

After the discussion has gone on long enough for everyone to state their beliefs and we can all see that there aren't any definite answers, then and only then do I state MY beliefs. And since I'm the teacher, they all listen.

"I tend to believe you have three levels of mind," I tell everyone. "There's your conscious mind, your own unconscious, and then the collective unconscious. In many ways, everyone here is right in their beliefs."

"Oh, come on," the older people say. "We can't ALL be right!"

I almost tell that person that HE is wrong, but I hold my tongue.

"Your conscious mind is the one you are using right now," I explain. "That chattering in your head as I speak is your conscious mind. It's thinking and you can hear it thinking.

"Below that is your personal unconscious mind," I go on. "It is deeper and slightly less accessible. It holds everything you ever did, saw, heard, or in any way sensed or experienced.

"And under that is the collective unconscious," I say. "It's our connection with each other and all things."

"So where's our mind?" someone asks.

"Your conscious mind is in your brain, your personal unconscious is in your body, and YOU are in the collective unconscious."

"Say what?" someone asks.

"What's all this have to do with writing?" someone else asks.

"I don't get it!" yet another person declares.

"Look," I begin, somewhat flustered. "You already know how to use your conscious mind. You're using it right now. I want you to use your personal unconscious next, because that is where you are carrying your most powerful stories."

"You mean my past is in my body?" a teenager asks.

"Exactly!"

"Wow!" most of the class exclaims.

"Bull!" an old-timer spits out. "My mind ain't in my body!"

So I decide to explain it all with a story.

"Years ago I had a Rolfing session....."

"A what?"

"A Rolfing session. It's a deep-tissue massage. You lie on a table and get your muscles ironed out by someone with real strong hands."

"Oh."

"While I was being Rolfed," I continue, "I began to remember things, stuff that I had long ago forgotten. As the Rolfer worked on my inner thighs, I remembered climbing a tree when I was four or five, and then falling out of it. It was as though my BODY had stored this memory in itself and the Rolfer unlocked it with his massage."

"Wow," some exclaim.

"Bull," a hold-out states. "That doesn't mean the memory was in your body."

"Maybe not," I say. "But this is my class and I say it does!"

Everyone laughs. They know I'm only kidding.

"Well, if my body is my unconscious mind, what good is knowing that?" a teenager asks.

"Great question!" I shout. "As a writer, you can tap the wisdom of your body for powerful new stories. As a person seeking transformation, you can pay attention to your body and unlock the stored memories there. When you clear your body, you clear your mind, and vice-versa."

"I get it!" a student says, eyes alive. "I might be walking in a certain way or carrying myself in an odd way because my body is holding stuff in it, which really means my MIND is holding stuff and it's showing up in my body."

"You got it!" I say.

"So how do we free our unconscious mind from this stuff in our body?"

"There are four ways that I know of right now," I explain. "First, you can do free-form writings where you pay attention to your feelings and write what you sense within yourself. Two, you can do Yoga, which will help loosen your mind and clear it. Three, you can practice the Option Process to locate the beliefs causing the feelings. And four, you can look into a new self-help technique called Focusing. Because I think that Focusing enhances the other methods, let's look at it."

"Okay," most of the class says.

FOCUSING

Ever wondered why therapy doesn't always work?

Eugene Gendlin did. He was a research psychologist at the University of Chicago assigned the awesome task of answering that very question. He listened to hundreds of taped therapy sessions until he pinpointed what was going on. Gendlin found that successful therapy didn't depend on the therapy, or on the therapist, but on something the patient did inside himself when in a session.

Gendlin found that successful therapy patients paid attention to their bodies in a unique way. They didn't just think about the session, they didn't just do whatever the therapist suggested. Rather, these particular patients were tuning in to how they felt in their bodies about the issues they were addressing. This way of listening, or focusing on a problem, facilitated change.

Gendlin narrowed this way of listening into a few simple steps and has been teaching this new form of therapy since the '70s. He wrote about it in a popular book called *Focusing*. Later on he applied his method to dream interpretation and wrote about that in a book titled *Let Your Body Interpret Your Dreams*. I have adapted Gendlin's method for my writing classes and am writing about it in a book called (for now, anyway) *Writing For Transformation*.

Here, very briefly, are the Focusing steps:

(1) Inventory what is on your mind

(2) Pick one issue to work on

(3) Put a handle on the feeling around the issue

(4) Be patient

In a nutshell, Focusing involves sitting with a problem until that problem speaks to you through your body. Give me a second to explain this. We are so used to thinking ABOUT problems that we never fully FEEL the problems. Focusing is like meditation. It encourages you to slow down and "sit with" your issue. If you are gentle and patient, that issue may open up and "speak" to you. When it does, you feel a release, a shift, a healing.

Let's use one of Gendlin's metaphors: Imagine yourself going on a trip. You've just boarded the plane and settled in your seat. Suddenly you realize you forgot something. But you can't recall just what you forgot. You know something is missing, you can sense it, but you aren't sure what. Your body tenses up as you go through your mental inventory. "Was it my wallet? No, I got it. Was it my ticket? No, got that, too. Was it my luggage. No, It's here." And--oh yes!--you quickly remember that you forgot your toothbrush! As you realize what you forgot, your body releases, your mind clears, and everything is okay again. You still don't have your toothbrush, mind you, but now you have experienced a shift about the whole issue and you feel better.

That's Focusing.

Here's a personal example: After I learned Focusing (from Gendlin's book, research papers, and his tape series), I decided to try it on something new. It was a Saturday morning and I faced numerous choices for what I could do. I decided to let my body guide me. I felt apprehensive as I began the process, but I sat there and allowed my body time. Listening to your mind is like sitting with a shy child. Yelling, being aggressive, being dominant, just doesn't work. You have to be there in a quiet, loving way, and WAIT for it to speak. Sometimes it speaks, sometimes it doesn't. You have to be willing to accept anything---including nothing at all.

After a few minutes I suddenly felt a shift in my body---like the aha! experience you get when you think of a new idea---and I knew that I wanted to go change the tires on the car.

Change the tires on the car? Sounds like an odd thing for my body to want to do. I could have vetoed that decision with my conscious mind. But somehow it felt right to take care of the car. So I did. And I have always remembered that event because of the clarity of purpose and the good feeling involved. It's as though I listened to a deeper part of me, a wiser part, and I was better off for it.

That's Focusing, too.

Here's one more example: I'm not always comfortable speaking in front of groups. Since that is America's number one fear, I imagine you aren't comfortable doing it either. But I recall one night, right before a class I was to teach, where my nervousness was making me sick. I decided to sit down and do Focusing.

I let myself fully experience my fears. And as I felt them in my body, I allowed my body the opportunity to speak. I cleared my mind.

I waited. After a minute or so a word came to me. It bubbled up from within me and I knew it was right.

Unfortunately I don't recall the word. But I clearly remember feeling better. Lighter. Happier. Stronger. Ready to go ahead and do the class. Just letting the discomfort speak to me helped me release it. From there I was ready to teach my class. And I did!

As much as I am fascinated by Focusing, I have some concerns about it. For one thing, they emphasize the body and seem to forget that the mind made the body. That is to say, your beliefs created your body. Change your beliefs and you change your body. If you have a stored memory in your body about falling out of a tree when you were three, it's there because of the beliefs you made at that moment of the event.

Focusing comes from the other direction. It says listen to your body and you free your body. It's the old chicken-and-egg question: Which came first, your thoughts or your feelings?

Does it matter?

MILTON WARD

Though Milton Ward never trained in Focusing, and in fact never heard of it until I told him about it, his unique blend of Yoga and body awareness seems akin to Gendlin's method.

"My books are a menace," Milton Ward told me over miso soup. We were in New York City and he was taking me to lunch across the street from the famed New York Open Center, where Ward and other teachers have introduced the public to new ideas.

"My books insist on being scratched on the nearest scrap of paper, and usually at four in the morning. They come more from my feelings than my figurings."

That figures. Milton Ward, now 71 (and in perfect health), has been listening to his "instinctual feelings," as he terms it, for several decades. He is the author of several plays and six books, the most popular being *The Brilliant Function of Pain*. In the latter he explained that pain is a gift, a "yogic guide" directing us back to our natural selves.

Ward is founder and president of the Milton Hood Ward Fund Campaign Company in New York City. In the last thirty years he has worked as a fundraiser for the government, major corporations, the Integral Yoga Institute, the Kripalu Center, and Elisabeth Kubler-Ross's center in Head Waters, Virginia. He recently founded The Instinctual Consciousness Institute to help people "return to pure feeling undisturbed by mind."

"I have been on the inside of many New Age groups," Ward told me. "I have watched Eastern philosophy become a major factor in the West. But the movement has become exploited. We have lost some of our open-hearted wisdom, our natural omniscience."

I didn't always understand Ward, but I enjoyed being with him. His quietness, his gentle, genuine smile, made me feel very comfortable. There was something about his trust in the ebb and flow of the universe that made me relax with him.

Born in the Bronx in 1917 of Russian Jewish immigrants (his father knew Lenin), Ward attributes his profound faith to the non-dualist philosophy of the East and the Jewish Kabbalah. He is an intensely spiritual person who believes in the quiet power of "mindless, intuitive feeling."

"I believe we organize and rationalize ourselves to exhaustion and rigor mortis," Ward told me. "We let our minds try to control everything when that is an impossibility."

That's why our relationships don't succeed, either.

127

"We think love more than we feel love," Ward writes in ***Feeling-Love***, his latest book. "We block and distort our pure feeling with our minds."

Ward openly told me he wrote the book because I had once encouraged him to write his autobiography. But Ward really wrote ***Feeling-Love*** out of a love-hate relationship. Love for the feeling-love in each of us, and hate for the idea that three out of every five marriages end in divorce. In ***Feeling-Love***, probably his most passionate and autobiographical work, Ward shares the tantra secrets that will guide us into feeling our centered, instinctual, pure love---our "language of consciousness." The book is divided into five sections and gently leads readers into restoring their capacity to feel authentic love.

"Psychologists tell us to trust our feelings," Ward tells me. "But we don't know how to feel our feelings. We'd sooner trust the latest book, pill, or medical opinion. This is the sickness of our time."

A 1940 graduate of Julliard, Ward married his music school sweetheart. They have been together fifty years. "We were once called up to see the Dean for kissing in a practice room," Ward says with a smile. He shares his relationship with his wife, Nona, an accomplished violinist, in ***Feeling-Love***. He writes, "For Nona and myself it has been our feeling-love that is the unquenchable source of our marriage."

"How do you return to your feeling-love?" I asked him.

"Practice," Ward replies. "If you feel tension in your chest right now, then focus on it. Listen to it. Feel it. It may be telling you to relax, to let go."

As Ward and I finished our meal, he looked at me and said, "It's really not so complicated. From feeling your physical body, you simply go deeper and begin to feel the love that is always there, always waiting, always wonderful. The miracle is going on right now. All you have to do is feel it."

I believe Ward is on the same track as Gendlin, but running in a deeper groove. Where Gendlin focuses on problems so you can transform them, Ward seems to be going deeper. He seems to be saying, "Listen to the life-force pump through you." Or, as guru Master Da Free John sometimes asks, "Who is beating your heart right now?" Ward and John are pointing at your essence.

WHICH CAME FIRST?

As much as I admire Gendlin and Ward and the other body-loving people I've met, I think there are certain limitations to their methods. For one thing, most of them entirely dismiss the mind. Ward says our egos can't grasp everything in any moment, and that we have to let go to something deeper in order to live. Gendlin uses the mind only to maintain focus on the body.

My own experience is that you need both. The body and mind are doors to the same truth. A combination would be much more powerful, and in all my counseling with people, I use an integrated method to tap the best of both worlds. But generally speaking I'd say beliefs are still the fundamental key to change. You either find the beliefs through your mind, or you find them through your body. The beliefs are what you are operating from. How you locate them is up to you.

I remember interviewing John and Kris Amodeo, Gendlin-trained Focusing teachers and authors of the book, *Being Intimate*. I watched their bodies move as I brought up certain subjects. John, for example, crossed his arms AND legs as I asked him about verbal methods for personal change. He was obviously defensive. His body and mind revealed it. His belief was that you had to work with the body in order to change, and he wasn't allowing anything else in.

Milton Ward and I sat in a taxi cab on the way to dinner and talked about the Option Process. He thought Barry Neil Kaufman had created a method to stay in the mind and out of the body. When I explained that people have emotional releases and body shifts in an

Option session, Ward visibly relaxed. He was glad to hear that Option wasn't another tool of the ego (like a tool of the devil).

Years ago I worked for a large oil company. During that time I read about Focusing, Option, and other new methods for personal growth. I also heard about something called "muscle response testing", or Behavior Kinesiology (BK).

The muscle response test (MRT) is a way to find out how your body feels. You stand with your left arm out from your body, as if you are pointing down the street. A partner stands in front of you and places one hand on your right shoulder, the other hand on your extended left arm. Then, while you consider what you want to eat for lunch, your partner gives a small push down on your arm. If your arm goes down a few inches, it means your body doesn't want the food you think you want. If your arm stays firm and only gives way a tiny bit, then your body has said okay, dump that food in.

I was fascinated with this method of testing the body. I asked my wife to "muscle test" me on everything in the house. Then I went to work and told anyone who would listen about the MRT, and how your body would never lie, that it knew more than we did.

Tony, a co-worker, asked me to try MRT on him. I agreed.

He stood up in his office. I stood before him. He put out his left arm. I put my hand on it. We were ready.

"Think of something you like," I said.

"Cookies."

Perfect, I thought. Cookies would definitely be rejected by his body. I tested his arm. It was strong!

"Think of something else," I said.

"Ice cream."

This will do it, I thought to myself. Ice Cream is not healthy for ANY body. I tested Tony's arm. Again it was strong!

"I don't get it," I said out loud.

"What's wrong?" Tony asked.

"Well, those foods ought to weaken your body. They make YOU stronger."

"Well, I like ice cream and cookies," Tony said. "MY favorite dessert is cookies-and-cream-flavored ice cream."

Suddenly I remembered a sure-fire way to make Tony test weak.

"Get you arm up," I ordered. He did. "Now think of--- sugar!"

"Okay," he said.

I tested his arm. It was STILL strong!

Finally I asked him, "Look, how do you feel about sugar?"

"It's great!" he said.

"You don't think it's damaging to your body?"

"Not at all."

And that was the key. While most of us believe sugar is bad, Tony didn't. When the average person is muscle-tested while thinking of sugar, they test weak because they believe sugar is bad for them. Tony, on the other hand, thought sugar, cookies, and ice cream were all fine. And that belief showed up in his body.

Option counselor Mandy Evans once did a group session where a woman complained, "This method won't help me! My feelings are trapped in my body and all this talk won't get them out!"

"How did the feelings get there?" Mandy gently asked.

The question stopped the woman in her tracks. Her body went rigid, then she began to shake. The group participants gathered around the woman and held her while her body twitched. After a long time the woman relaxed. She had chosen to release those pent-up feelings in that workshop. And she realized every feeling had taken hold in her physical structure based on the beliefs she had decided to have in her life.

Beliefs take hold in the body when we choose the belief. You may have chosen the belief in the second grade, or last week. But once you accept it, it becomes part of your appearance. It goes into your personal unconscious, and since your personal unconscious is in your body, it can be seen (by experts) in your body. To change that belief you either have to pay attention to your body, or pay attention to your mind. Focusing is one way to heed the body. Option is one way to heed the mind. They don't conflict, they complement.

If I've learned anything in my twenty-year trek through personal-growth seminars and workshops, book and tapes, it's that everything fits. For the longest time I believed Freud was off his cigar and Jung was God. Those psychological God-figures never seemed to agree, and I chose one over another.

But then I read a wonderful book by the transpersonal genius, Ken Wilber, called *No Boundary*. What Ken explained is that the various paths to growth---including old Freud and dreamy Jung---were complementary, not conflicting. They were like rungs on a ladder. Every rung is needed to get to the top.

Focusing and Option are similar rungs. Depending on which you are attracted to, either will work. Option is dialogue-oriented. Focusing is inner-directed. But let the body/mind system speak. Both facilitate change. Both are based in love and respect.

Isn't that the ideal path to follow?

Chapter Nine

THE ROAD MOST TRAVELLED

I've done many workshops and seminars. Too many, maybe. I spent two weekends in a locked room with Werner Erhard's people and two summers with a controversial guru. I've seen my past lives, been re-birthed and hypnotized, done deep breathing and meditation, and I've walked on hot coals. All of it was unique. None of it was very practical.

But then I took a five-week course called "Technologies For Creating" (TFC) which deepened my understanding of myself as a writer. It also gave me new tools to create the life I wanted. It impressed me more than any other course I had ever taken. If nothing else, it was easy, fun, and practical.

TFC: YOU ARE THE CAPTAIN ON YOUR SHIP

TFC is a course created by Robert Fritz, author of the 1984 bestseller, *The Path of Least Resistance*. Fritz has recently rewritten his course and seventy percent of his book. Why? As this playful,

46-year-old musician told me over the phone, "I finally learned how to write!"

Fritz is not an advocate of the "New Age." He finds most of it self-deceiving. In his book he has a long section exploding the myth of positive thinking. For Fritz, positive thinking is simply a way to lie about reality to make it seem better. I know many people who talk about "canceling negative thoughts" and "only think positive." Fritz says you can be honest with yourself and still move forward toward your goals.

"All of these systems still work within the same structure," Fritz told me. "You end up going back and forth between what you want and what you think you have and you never truly change. In order to create results, you have to change the dominant structure at play in your life."

That's often easier said than done. But Fritz's ideas make sense. I have seen many seekers dismiss their current reality by focusing only on what they want. They believe that just visualizing the end result will make it happen. Imagery is one step in the process, but only ONE step. Knowing where you're at now, as Fritz points out, gives you an energy to go forward to create the result you want.

Since 1975 more than 100,000 people, including NASA officials, politicians, and singer Phoebe Snow, have taken various seminars created by Fritz. More than 60,000 have graduated from his TFC course. More than 80,000 bought his original book.

"I teach people how to use the creative process," Fritz told me. "I've taken what I've learned from composing music and from the lives of the great artists, and I've applied the same principles to other areas of life."

Fritz's course and book are fundamentally about each individual becoming "the predominate creative force in your life."

"That doesn't mean you are the creative force in the universe," Fritz explained to me. "But you are the creative force in your own life. And that's vastly different from what most people do."

Most of us bounce off circumstances by reacting to them. Fritz teaches you to choose how you want to be in the world. This change in perspective creates an amazing sense of empowerment.

"Once you begin to choose the results you'd like to have, you create different structures in your life," Fritz said. "Your energy and life will then follow through the path of the new structure, the path of least resistance."

You probably keep on getting the same results in your life because you keep on doing the same things. That's called being stuck in a structure. Or "oscillating." Or just being stupid. Fritz says you will oscillate between conflicting wants until you learn how to create a new, more dominate path. The best way I can describe this is to point out that people who diet oscillate between eating and not eating, dieting and not dieting. But if you decide to run a marathon or become a model, you change the structure and you naturally lose weight as you move down the path to your new goal: winning that marathon or being a top model. Rather than fighting the battle of wanting to eat versus wanting to diet, you step beyond it into the field of wanting something larger and better than before. It's the difference between going for peanuts and going for the gold.

Interviewing Fritz was a struggle. I wanted to know how to create specific results and Fritz talked about Mozart. I wanted to know how he taught reactive-responsive people to be more creative, and he said he didn't do that. In desperation I finally asked Fritz, "How do we create ANYTHING in life using the principles in your book?"

"Everyone wants a formula," Fritz replied. "In the creative process you make up what you need to do to create what you want. There are no rules."

People reacting to life seek how-to's so they know how to better respond to circumstances. But a person in charge of his destiny "invents" his own path. As Fritz told me, "The creative process is a learning process."

CREATING RESULTS

I was amazed at how gentle the TFC course is. After doing the Forum and other confrontative seminars, the laid-back atmosphere of my TFC group seemed like a kindergarten class at naptime.

The course is simple. You sit around the room with your other class members (I had four others) and take turns reading from the giant course notebook. In between there are "techniques," which are guided visualizations, that the TFC certified instructor guides you through. There is also a lot of writing time where you list your goals and consider the direction of your life.

We were asked to pick 13 goals for our life and to focus on one of them. I picked heavy-duty targets. I figured I paid $300 for the course, I wanted my money's worth. I didn't pick wimpy goals like "I want a new suit." Rather, I chose big-ticket items like a better relationship with my father, a career as a speaker, finding a major publisher for one of my self-published books, a new house, a new Mercedes. Little things like that.

We were asked to read our list of goals twice a day and to listen to one of the four sides of our tapes every day. The tape takes only ten minutes so it isn't a problem. (One woman did the tapes while driving to work, which isn't a good idea.) All it does is relax you, help you focus, and then visualize your goal while also visualizing your current reality in relation to that goal. Fritz claims that the combination of the two creates a "structural tension" that naturally seeks resolution.

He's right. One of the greatest benefits I got from TFC was understanding this "structural tension." All of my published works have been short. I never knew why. I just thought I was a concise writer. But I learned that I didn't like the tension between having a vision and wanting a desired result. I would write my stuff as fast as I could and stop. I wanted to get rid of the tension. I have since learned that tension is a needed and wonderful ally. Now I can write longer works and really enjoy the process. That alone is a priceless gift for me.

For several weeks I focused on getting a large advance for ***Turbocharge Your Writing!***, my writing booklet. Fritz and everyone else said "Don't focus on the money, focus on the end result. Money is a process." And I'd say, "I know, I know, but I want the money!"

This went on for weeks. Then I went into a bookstore and saw a paperback that was the size and feel of what I imagine ***Turbo*** will be when it is republished. I bought that book. I began to use it in my imagery sessions. I'd see my name and my book's title on the cover and I'd see my current reality (the booklet as it is now) at the same time.

Within two days I got a phone call from a major New York publishing house. The editor there had heard of my ***Turbo*** booklet and wanted to see it. Who was she? The very editor who had published the book I bought and was using in my visualizations!

Coincidence? Maybe. And maybe we are linked on a level we aren't even aware of. Who knows? As Fritz said on a radio interview, "You don't need to know how it works for it to work." Indeed.

One day, as I was reading my list of 13 goals, I realized I had created two of them without knowing it. It had happened so naturally I didn't even see it coming. As I read my list and saw the one about my father, it dawned on me that my Dad and I were talking more. And more openly. And more often. He was taking a more candid interest in my latest book. He acted, sometimes, like a press agent for the book. And I noticed I was dealing with him in an authentic way. This was not focused on. As my TFC instructor later said, "The other goals are happening as you work on your primary one." Indeed.

Another goal was to be a speaker. Without trying, I got offers to give talks. One in Houston led to two more in Houston. Then the Romance Writers Guild wanted me to speak in San Antonio. And in California. ANY offer from them is a shock since I have never written a romance novel.

Next I got an offer from Australia to speak and teach over there. I was stunned. I had not contacted ANY of these places. Yet the offers for talks were coming in. One class member said, "When you tell the universe what you want, stand back. It's on its way." Indeed.

A side benefit I got from the course was more effective consulting. I was still working on *The Joy of Service* with Ron McCann while taking TFC. I was seeing him every day. One day he began to complain about his business. Though he has a multi-million dollar air-conditioning repair business, he wanted more. (Don't we all?) I listened to him because I knew this was his current reality. It is good to know where you are before you go forward. Your current reality is the first part of the equation that helps you reach success.

But when I said "What do you want?", Ron began to describe his ideal company. Sometimes he'd say such-and-such isn't possible. I'd say, "Don't worry about what's possible. Describe your ideal vision." And I walked him through the process until he felt comfortable and complete with his vision.

Then I rushed out the door. Why? Because I knew he would want to know what to DO next and I couldn't tell him. He'd have to let his vision bring that up to him. It's hard to explain but there isn't a WAY, a method, a formula, to get anything. If you know where you want to go, and you know where you are, you know what to do next. It's natural. When I wanted to be a speaker, people said I had to join the National Speaker's Association. Well, obviously I didn't have to do that. As Fritz told me over the phone one day, "We're dealing with creativity here. There is no single way to create what you want. You make it up as you go along."

A week later Ron reported that he created the company he wanted. He was smiling. I was shocked. It was an amazing side benefit from my doing the TFC course. Ron was so grateful that he came to my TFC graduation as a way of saying thank-you to me and to the course. He knew he owed his new company to the Fritz material.

HEALING OR CURED?

Many people into self-discovery and personal growth find it fashionable to be co-dependant, or addictive, or the offspring of an alcoholic.

One friend constantly talks about his past. He seems most alive when he can complain about what happened to him when he was abused as a child. A script he is writing begins with "I am a sex addict...."

I keep hearing people in the New Age say "You create your own reality." I also keep seeing these people botch their lives. I believe that they are somewhat off the mark. Many New Agers do their affirmations and visualizations but forget that they aren't invincible. Death will get us all. It humbles the mightiest. But yet many in the New Age act as if they are immune to the realities of life. They work on healing themselves but forget that healing isn't curing. A cure is total remission; healing is peace with the problem.

Fritz's focus is on cured. He asks you to decide on what you want, and then he teaches you the skills to create what you want. You don't have to investigate your past or heal old wounds or write plays about your past illnesses, either. When you make a structural change, everything changes---your past, your beliefs, your attitudes, your problems---everything!

"How can my past change in an instant?" a friend asked.

"I'll explain it to you in a revealing way," I began. "When I tried to lose weight last year, I did it by fighting with food. When I didn't eat, I thought about eating. When I did eat, I thought about not eating. I kept wondering if I needed to change my beliefs, or deal with parent-child issues, or have a past-life experience."

"I can relate to that," he said.

"But there was a time, back when I was about 17, when I decided to be the heavyweight boxing champion of the world.I was sincere and dedicated. I worked out every day, ran, punched the bag, and visualized myself as the champion. There was never a concern about eating or not eating. It was no longer an issue. The entire fat-thin problem dropped with a single decision to go for something more."

What I had done was change my structure. Rather than live within a frame that said my choices were "eat or not eat," I changed the picture to "Go for the heavyweight title."

Fritz's method is a short-cut to health. You don't have to play with your illness or focus on your past (though you can, if you want.) All you really have to do is choose to go for what you want.

This is a tough idea for many people to accept. They still believe that you only grow through pain, that you only change through suffering, that you can only alter the present by examining the past.

Not so.

SELLING

One complaint with TFC---and with most New Age, personal-growth seminars---concerns the people who sell it. One of the Houston instructors, for example, is a pushy salesperson. She doesn't seem to realize that different paths are for different people at different times. For her, it's "my way or no way."

I've learned that each of us is on a unique schedule of growth. TFC may not be for everyone. To have a salesperson say TFC will transform your life is to make a disrespectful statement. The TFC instructor in Houston won't support anyone who isn't into self-healing and self-growth. I think that is cruel and disrespectful of a person's personal power and personal freedom.

Some people learn more from being stuck than they do moving forward. So why not let them be where they choose to be?

Even Mark Twain knew better. He saw that what worked for him--namely cigars and profanity---may annihilate you.

It's the same problem with most self-help courses. Werner Erhard's are notorious for their hard-sell approach. My belief is that all of these people need to understand that the basis of all selling is true friendship. Most of these salespeople are coming from a place of self-righteousness, and that is as primitive and ignorant as the worst religious tribes---and the cause of the ugliest wars---in our world's history.

The strategy of most New Age selling is to set up a need and then fill it with what they are selling.

"Are you unhappy? Ill? Tried? Broke? In a funk?" they ask you. "Relationship problems? Work problems? Not sure of your purpose or direction?"

Any variation of the above will help them establish the fact that you NEED a cure, an answer, a path, etc.

"Just do this course and it'll all clear up!!"

I remember going to an introduction to "est" about ten years ago. An attractive young woman pulled me aside after the talk and said, "When do you want to sign up?"

"I don't have the money," I said.

"Do you want more money, Joe?"

"Yes."

"Do you want a better job?"

"Yes."

"Do you want a girlfriend?"

"I'm married."

"Do you want a better relationship?" she asked. "Take the est course and your whole life will change."

A man who does the firewalk thinks the answer to everything is walking on hot coals. I remember talking to him on the phone one day. I was complaining about my situation in life. He listened for a moment and then started making sounds like a crackling fire.

"What you need is a firewalk!" he announced.

Later, when this same man grew more interested in Breath Therapy than firewalking, he would say, "What you need is a breath session!"

The last-ditch tactic for all of these mediocre salespeople is to say, "Are you afraid to do the class?"

A variation of this same trick is the statement, "You don't have to be afraid. The class is safe."

None of it is enlightened selling. All of it is based on the idea that you don't know and they do. Though Fritz's people are not as pushy as Erhard's, there is still a single-mindedness involved that is not holistic.

THE ACCESS POINT

TFC is great. But what if something goes wrong? What if you have a setback? Or you get depressed?

I'm glad you asked. Fritz has a wondrous technique called the Access Point. I've used this one a lot. A while back I was told I was going to be on the cover of a major national magazine. I was interviewed, photographed. The works. But then I was dropped from the line-up for that issue. I was devastated. I was depressed. I was suicidal. I had counted on that national publicity. Now what was I going to do?

And then I remembered the Access Point technique. It has four steps to it and goes like this:

Step one: What was I telling myself about this situation? That I was no good, that the magazine was no good, that life was no good. And so on.

Step Two: Is this what you want to create? NO way! I didn't want to create myself as "no good" or the magazine or my world as "no good."

Step three: What do you WANT to create? I wanted to feel good about myself and my work and my world.

Step four: Choose what you want to create. I chose to feel good about myself and my work and my world.

I immediately felt better. You may not understand it, but the Access Point switches your focus so you are more in control. More creative. You choose where you want to go and how you want to feel. It's better than being a victim. And once you switch into being the predominate creative force in your life, you ACT differently.

After I did the above, I got on the phone with the magazine writer who had interviewed me. He apologized for my story's being dropped. But he said he had a national radio show and he'd like to interview me on it!

So the Access Point helped me move from being depressed and even suicidal to feeling more powerful and even getting further publicity for myself.

THE POWER OF CHOICE

One day I told myself I was going to have a good day. This was on a Saturday, a notoriously lousy day for me. Usually all I seem to do on Saturdays is play chauffeur and drive my wife around Houston as she shops and runs errands. I never enjoy it. But this day I CHOSE to have fun. I simply chose to enjoy the day.

Not only did the day become a wonderful memory for me, it became a prime example of the power of choice. Even my wife noticed the difference. She said, "You seem different."

"How so?" I asked.

"You seem happy," she said. "Like you're really enjoying this."

I laughed. I never told her what I had done. All I did was choose to have a wonderful day. It seems too simple to work. But it does. It did. My TFC instructor once told the story of how a student walked onto the green and chose to have a great game of golf. She then proceeded to play her best game ever.

Choosing works. So choose what you want for yourself. Once you do, entire unknown forces come into play to help you get what you want.

YOUR TWO QUESTIONS

A friend of mine called me the other day before leaving on a trip to the mountains. He was going to spend a week in solitude reflecting on his life. He wanted to know what I thought were the most important questions for him to ask himself.

"There are two major ones," I told him.

"Let me write them down."

"The first is `Where am I now?' and the second is `What do I want for myself?'"

"Where am I now and what do I want next?" he repeated. "Okay, I got it."

"The first helps you know where you are in your life. You have to be honest with yourself in answering it. It's real easy to lie and make your life look better or even worse than what it really is. You have to look at it nonjudgmentally and just read off what you see."

"Okay," he said.

"And knowing what you want is important because you can't get anywhere without direction. Since you can make your life what you want, what do you want? If you could have anything in the world, or be anything, what would you have or be? Don't worry about what's possible. Just create your vision of what you want for you."

"State what I want for me," he said. "I got it."

"The combination of the two creates a tension that seeks resolution," I explained. "You can only get that resolution by either giving up or getting your goal."

"So never give up," he said.

"Exactly. Never, ever, ever, ever give up."

He understood. He took my shortened version of Fritz's TFC course to the mountains. He reflected on his life and where he wanted to go. And he came back and started his own publishing company. Though his road is rough, he is now creating one of Houston's hottest and most reliable new business magazines.

THE BIRTH OF A DREAM

Here's one last example of the power of creativity:

I was having lunch with a friend. I was telling him about my new business idea and he was playing the role of devil's advocate (playing it real well, too).

"The Writing Institute will be for everyone who wants to write," I said, bursting with enthusiasm for my project. "There will be several classrooms, a place for staged readings of plays, a bookstore, an office, a placement service, and a mail-order catalog for software and other unique items."

"Have you written a business plan?"

"Yep. Finishing it right now."

"So you want to create this and you don't have any experience, you don't have any money, you don't have any customers, and the idea has never been done before?"

"That pretty well sums it up," I said.

"I don't think it has a chance."

"Look, my friend," I said. "You are basing everything you said on the past, on probability, not possibility. You are looking at the past to predict the future. Most of the time that sort of thinking will give you accurate results because most of us repeat the past until we die. But not this time."

"Why not this time?" he asked.

"What I am doing is creating something new, something so unique and special that it has NEVER been done before! You can't compare it to the past since my idea is new. I am creating something, not duplicating something."

I'm not sure he understood. But I certainly did. I knew that I was molding a dream and that any references to the past were pointless. I was creating. What most people do is find out what works and copy it. I see writers examining the *New York Times* bestseller list to see what will be a hit. Problem is that list tells you what WAS a hit, not what will be a bestseller. You have to come from creativity in order to create the results you envision.

And creativity is the heart of Robert Fritz's course.

THE POWER OF YOUR HAND

But Fritz's course is not complete. He's left out a few essential steps. And apparently he left them out intentionally.

Right now I am working on a short book called **The Power of Your Hand**. It is about a five-step formula for creating results in your life. The title refers to the fact that you must use your hand---take action---in order to create results. And the title also gives you a way to remember my system: one step for each finger of your hand.

Let me give you a short course in my "Power of Your Hand" system. These steps will illustrate where I think Fritz is right on---and where I think he is lacking.

Step One: What do you want?

Fritz agrees that you have to know what you want before you can create it. But he's not of much help when it comes to tuning in on what you want. He says, "Make it up!" But most of us don't know how to make it up. We don't know what we want. In my system I use a number of techniques to help you get clear on your desires. Fritz doesn't. He just says, "Decide on what you want." Easy to say, but not to do.

Step Two: Do you believe you can do it (or have it)? Fritz says it doesn't matter what you believe or how you feel. Like a sick person who goes to work anyway, Fritz says you can create no matter what. He's right in the sense that you can still be productive even if you're feeling out of sorts. But he's wrong in the sense that what you believe CAN either help you or stop you. My experience has proven that if a person doesn't believe they can do something, they won't do it.

One of Fritz's own TFC instructors keeps creating classes with only a handful of people in them. Until she explores her beliefs and her sense of self-worth, she's going to keep creating small classes. Fritz doesn't address these core issues at all. It's a black hole where all his students fall.

Step Three: Are you willing to do whatever it takes?

Fritz agrees that persistence is important. His Access Point technique is a wonderful way to keep on track. Fritz encourages a "never give up" attitude. His system has this step covered completely.

Step Four: Are you willing to accept something better?

Too many people in the New Age look at obstacles as signs to give up. In my opinion the "signs" can be messages to try HARDER, not give up. But the message may also be to consider accepting something better. Fritz doesn't talk much about this issue. He assumes you know what you want (step one) and urges you to keep going until you get it. But I have to acknowledge that his focus on reality helps you check to see if you are being offered something better.

Step Five: Can you be happy now?

Fritz flunks this step. He says happiness is too nebulous to be a goal. He also says happiness comes and goes so don't focus on it. Again, I disagree. People like Wayne Dyer and Barry Neil Kaufman have proven that happiness is NOW and that it is a choice. In fact, when you are happy, you can better see what you want and what to do next. Also, being happy, or grateful, helps magnetize you to create more of what you want. Again, Fritz dismisses this step entirely.

All in all, Fritz tends to focus on results. My own experience with the creative process tells me that results are just one step in the process. After you create what you want, what then? You go on to the next vision. The whole experience is a cycle. Once you realize it is ALL a process, then you can relax and enjoy every step in the journey.

Fritz's ideas are powerful and they DO get results. But his ideas are also incomplete. Balance them with a feeling of moment-to-moment happiness and you will be on your way to what I'll call "practical spirituality"---the ability to be happy while creating heaven on earth.

Chapter Ten

BUSINESS: THE GREATEST GURU

How do you make money and still honor your inner self? Business is considered anti-spiritual for most seekers of truth. Trying to fit money into an Eastern and Western synthesis of values is a primary source of confusion and frustration.

In the last few years I have come to realize that the business world is the greatest arena for personal transformation. In business you have to face your fears, transcend your ego, and learn to live beyond limits, all while doing your best to hear and heed the call from within. The pay-offs and risks are greater, too. In business you can get rich. But you can also die broke and miserable.

VISITING MARRS

How you respond to an event in the business world is your test of strength and wisdom. For Donald Marrs, once a top executive for one of the largest advertising firms in the world, that test came in many forms. There was a divorce, profound unhappiness on the job, and an inner prompt to dump everything he worked for, uproot and move, and try another road. Despite negative responses from family, friends and co-workers, Marrs had the courage to give in to his dream of writing screenplays in Hollywood.

But following inner guidance doesn't guarantee immediate material success. Marrs faced harsh setbacks and severe disappointments. His scripts were read but not bought. He landed lush jobs at 20th Century Fox and Disney, but lost both in humiliating ways. Still, Marrs wanted to trust his new friend, the inner voice within him. And he knew that any spiritual path had to be workable on the material plane to be valid.

"If there was a God and a path of discovery, it had to lead right through the marketplace of the world as well as through the deserts," Marrs writes in his warm autobiography, *Executive in Passage*.

"It felt anti-life to deny the earth when it was where I lived."

As a creative writer in the advertising world Marrs had learned to trust his feelings about ideas, and this led him to great success. But in daily life he let his rational self make the decisions. Now, slowly, and sometimes very painfully, he was learning to trust a new way of knowing. He was gradually becoming aware that he could listen to and follow his desires and passions at all times, not just on the job.

"The way forward came from simply following what excited me," Marrs writes, "and as I did, I slowly became aware that the clues appeared more and more often."

Marrs gradually became aware of a "Subtle Agenda," as he calls it, guiding his life. To understand what was happening to him Marrs began to see life as a metaphor. He would spend long periods by his pool interpreting daily events by sensing how they felt in his body. In short, Marrs was being led to an opening of his heart. He was learning to let go of his fears and discovering that underneath his worst nightmares was "...a realm of loving security...a wholeness I'd never known existed."

Marrs continued to struggle with financial concerns, however. His worry over shrinking funds drained his energy until he let go of his last two attachments, a stray dog who taught him how to love again (who sadly died of cancer), and a large house which Marrs adored. But the result of releasing these concerns was the birth of a subtle craving, both new and surprising, to go back into advertising, but this time as head of his own small company. Consequently he created Marketing Partners, Inc., a firm dedicated to high ideals, strong values and to serving small businesses.

"After I sold my house and went through the experiences I described in my book," Marrs told me by phone one day, "I have made more money, had more fun, found a bigger and better house which I adore, and have established a wonderful relationship with a woman I love."

Marrs' story fits with my experiences. It shows that following our loving inner desires works in the business world. There is no need to separate business from spirituality. Both work quite well together, as Marrs will attest. He says that you will not have to go through the calamities he did if you listen to your inner messages. "Resisting these signals only postpones what might have been a relatively smooth transformation, and instead magnifies a minor tremor into a significant earthquake."

I remember a popular teacher telling a group of businesspeople that if they ignore their inner promptings to change, those nudges will turn into something more attention-getting, like ulcers or cancer.

MYSTIC IN THE MARKETPLACE

Ram Dass used to tell a story about his relationship to money that is very enlightening---but not for the reasons you may first think.

Dass had created some sort of recording and was selling them for, we'll say, $4.50 each. His father, a very money-oriented man, asked Dass how much profit he was making.

"It costs $4 to make the tape, so we make about fifty cents."

"If you charged more per tape, would you still sell as many tapes?"

"Probably. The people buying them would pay up to ten or twelve dollars each for them."

"Then why in the world aren't you charging more and making a bigger profit?"

Ram Dass thought a moment. He turned to his Dad and asked, "Remember when you did some work for Uncle Harry?"

"Of course. It took a lot of time and effort to prepare his case, but I did it."

"How much did you charge him?"

"Charge him? I didn't charge him anything. I did it all for nothing!"

"Why?" Ram Dass asked. "You could have made a nice profit."

"Why, he was my brother! He's YOUR uncle! I couldn't make a profit off him. He's family!"

"Well, everyone is my uncle," Ram Dass said. "Find someone who isn't a member of my family and I'll make a profit off him."

Sounds good, doesn't it? Sounds holy and spiritual. But is it practical?

I think Ram Dass, as wonderful a soul as he is, missed something. One friend listened to the above story and said, "You know, that story actually contributes to my poverty consciousness. It makes me devalue myself and my work."

One of the powerful thoughts that I got from my years with Rajneesh was that you could "meditate in the marketplace." Rajneesh saw capitalism as a wise way of life.

He saw money as the blood circulating in a healthy society. It encouraged you to create and it rewarded you when you created something people could use. In a very real way, Rajneesh helped me become a "Mystic In The Marketplace."

If you give away your work, several things happen: People receiving your work don't appreciate it unless there is a price tag on it; you can't create high-quality work because you don't have the funds to contribute to your resources; you begin to lose value for yourself as well as your work.

I wrote a book on service for Houston businessman Ron McCann. When Ron and I were beginning to negotiate our business, he asked me if I was going to charge him in advance to write his book.

"My service to you is to write your book for you," I explained to him. "Your service to me is to pay me for what I do."

There it is. No ego involved. No messy manipulative attempts to cheat anyone. Simply put, I'll do this for you and you do this for me. At one point in our planet's history this whole transaction stuff was done through bartering. You give me five furs and I give you two guns. That sort of thing.

And even today I find bartering to be a valid way to exchange energy. Again, when Ron McCann and I were talking about co-creating his book, *The Joy of Service*, I told him I'd write the book in exchange for a car. I knew as a company president he had several vehicles. Since I was going to use the money he was going to pay me to buy a car anyway, I suggested trading my work for a car.

You have to charge people for what you do, and you are entitled to a nice profit. The profit keeps you going. Walt Disney said he didn't make movies to make money, he made money so he could keep making movies. Think about it.

I used to write résumés for friends. I never charged anything. Like Ram Dass, I figured everyone was my uncle. But then I took a part-time job where I wrote executive résumés for a résumé-writing business. I was now getting up to $300 a résumé! And what I noticed is that people appreciated me more and liked their résumés better.

Barry Neil Kaufman, when he was first practicing the Option Process, would give away his time to anyone seeking his help. But people would skip appointments or come in late. They didn't value his work. Now Kaufman charges $125 an hour for an Option session and more than $1,000 a week for an intensive. And he has more business than he can handle.

One friend of mine called a few weeks ago. He wanted me to review his writing. Since he was "family," I said I'd do it for free. He said he'd be by the next day and we'd have lunch. He didn't show. He called later and said he'd drop the article off that evening. He never showed. The next day he called and said he would be right over. I waited. He didn't show. Finally he called in the afternoon and said he was coming right over.

"Don't bother," I said to him. "If you want me to read that article of yours, I'm gonna charge you to do it."

There was a long silence on the line.

"It's the only way I know to make you value my time and skills," I explained.

"I don't blame you at all," he said.

My relationship with him strengthened as a result of my honesty and his understanding.

SPY magazine once sent small checks to the wealthiest mega-stars to see if the celebrities would cash them. The larger checks were about $1.50. If the star cashed that check, *SPY* sent them an even smaller check. Only two people signed the checks that were under a dollar. One was Donald Trump, the billionaire.

It seems that even the wealthiest people on earth have the sense to count their cents.

DO WHAT YOU LOVE – AND THEN SELL IT!

There's a lot of talk these days about "Do what you Love and the money will follow."

Will it?

First, I think if you do ANYTHING at all in this society, money will follow. The question is how much money will follow and how long will it take to catch up with you. (Will it arrive in time to pay the electric bill?) I've seen beggars in downtown Houston make a living by holding out their hand. You can do just about anything and money will eventually come your way. It's the nature of our system.

But if you do what you love, will money follow? There was a wonderful article in a recent issue of *YOGA JOURNAL* magazine that examined the whole issue. In essence, the mantra doesn't hold true unless you add more phrases to it--- "Do what you love AND balance your checkbook AND be dedicated AND be persistent and then maybe money will follow" is more apt.

Let's put a sharper focus on this whole issue. I believe you have to do what you love in order to be happy and healthy in life. I further believe that you have to do what you love so well that people will buy what you've done. So I've created a new phrase:

"Do what you love and then sell it!"

I had to spend many years learning the craft of writing before anyone thought I was skilled enough to be worth any money. If you love writing, learn the art. Study. Practice. Work at it. Keep persisting, keep learning, and soon you will be in a position where you can make money from what you love.

Mark Twain's advice to writers was to work at a newspaper for two years---at no charge. If the paper didn't hire you after that, Twain said, become a carpenter.

If you want to be a dancer, the same premise holds true. There's a certain apprenticeship that has to take place before anything you love to do becomes a money-maker. Someone who longs to be a therapist doesn't just advertise in the Yellow Pages and become successful. Even Milton Erickson, probably the greatest hypnotherapist of all time, had to face ridicule and constantly work at his craft before he became successful. It doesn't happen overnight, no matter how many times you affirm "Do what you love and the money will follow."

Let me give you one more example.

THE MOST SUCCESSFUL YOGA TEACHER

The most successful Yoga teacher in the country may be Lex Gillan, the founder of The Yoga Institute and New Age Bookshop in Houston. Lex is a soft-spoken, gentle, bearded fellow who is dedicated to doing what he loves---and he's business-minded enough to make what he loves pay off.

Lex teaches seven levels (beginner through advanced) of raja and hatha Yoga classes and has an average of 500 (that's right, five hundred) students every six weeks. No other Yoga teacher has that many students. But Lex also runs the New Age Bookshop in his comfortable store in central Houston, sponsors many nationally known Yoga teachers for weekend events, spends several weeks a year in meditation at different monasteries, and still finds time for his wife and ten-month-old son.

Gillan is a former competitive weight trainer who won numerous awards for his power-lifting competition. He dumped his weight-training career, his trophies and more than one hundred pounds by studying Yoga. This was nearly twenty years ago.

"I was unhappy as a 250-pound athlete," he says. "I was tired of consuming two pounds of red meat and two gallons of milk a day."

But the real turning point for Lex came when he was fired from his job as a banker in 1974. That was the event that helped Lex move into doing what he loves on a full-time basis. He took $800 of his last one thousand, bought thirty days' worth of advertising in Houston newspapers, and opened The Yoga Institute.

"Being fired was a blessing," Gillan said. "I never had the courage to go out on my own before it."

He says his five years of experience in the bank's commercial credit department, and his degree in business, helped him make his Institute prosperous. So that's where Lex learned the craft of running a business.

"Just being consistent has helped my business," he explained. Far too many Yoga teachers move with the wind. Not Lex. "I've been in the same location since 1974."

Lex works very hard to keep his business simple.

"If you give people too many choices, their decision is no decision," Gillan explained. "All I teach is Yoga and teaching is still the greatest joy for me."

Lex rises at 4 every morning and is at his store by 5 a.m. He makes telephone calls to potential students whenever he is not waiting on bookstore customers, and maintains (with the help of his sister,

Greta) an active mailing list of more than 10,000 names. He has two part-time employees to help him run his 4,000-volume bookshop. Lex works an average of 80 hours a week and teaches all his Yoga classes himself.

What is the result of all this work? Gillan says he has taught more than 8,000 Yoga classes to more than 30,000 people, which may make his practice the most successful in the country.

"I love what I do," Gillan said.

What are his plans for himself and The Yoga Institute?

"I don't think like that," Gillan explained. "I never plan my life more than six weeks in advance. I like what I do and I'll just keep on doing it."

And no doubt he will continue to prosper and grow. Why? Because Lex is doing what he loves---and he knows how to sell what he does.

FOLLOW YOUR INNER COMPASS

Joseph Campbell is credited with saying, "Follow your bliss." I like the phrase. Short and sweet and filled with meaning.

I have always followed my passion. When I read about a man who cured himself of blindness, I grew excited and wrote him. The result was a mesmerizing interview with Meir Schneider---and a cover story article for *EAST WEST* magazine and inclusion in the book, ***Meetings With Remarkable Men and Women***.

When my years of fascination with writing and meditation merged into something that I was passionate about, I sat down and wrote ***Zen and the Art of Writing***---which became my first book.

When my love for books led me to discover the works of Alan Cohen, I was delighted. And my bliss from reading him turned into my reviews about his books, my finally meeting him---and my helping him edit his book *The Healing of the Planet Earth*.

When following my interests led me to pick up a harmonica, I went with my urges. It took one full year of daily practice and many books and tapes, but now I play whatever I feel on the harp and I've even written my first song---which was published!

And when my excitement for the works of William Saroyan turned into a desire to write a one-act comedy about him, I went with it. The result was a play I still love---and which was produced in Houston in 1979.

I could go on.

Mandy Evans, a wonderful, delightful Option Method counselor in San Diego, says we each have an "inner compass" to help us find our way. That inner compass, Mandy says, is "your own wanting."

Buddha supposedly said "Desire is the cause of all suffering." What Buddha actually said, according to Mandy, was "Misunderstood desire is the cause of all suffering." There's a major difference.

Desire is your inner sense of direction, says Mandy. "This system of navigation eliminates regret and guilt," she writes in *Emotional Options*, her first book. It's when your desire becomes a need, or an attachment, that you develop emotional suffering in the form of anger, fear, sadness, or guilt.

I believe we always know what we want, what excites us, what makes us vibrant and alive and happy. The catch is we don't always admit what we want to ourselves. Sometimes I get cranky and easily angered if I haven't had enough sleep. In those moments, if I am honest with myself, I simply ask, "What do I want?" And if I'm honest, I know I need a nap.

Following your bliss is the same. You know what excites you. You know what your bliss is. Somewhere in you is a little child who wants to come out and play. What makes you bubble up with laughter? What delights you?

Victor Dishy, in his wonderful book ***Inner Fitness***, suggests you "Follow Your Fascination." Dishy, a self-made millionaire, advocates what he calls "Applied Spirituality." He suggests you follow your "fascination," and to do it in a way that is practical.

You need to keep in mind that money is never the focus of following your passion. Financial success comes as a by- product of being true to yourself and expressing your love for something. Dishy says, "Follow your fascination and YOU will become fascinating; your joy and vibrancy will become contagious."

A friend of mine---a very wealthy publisher in Texas---says, "There is the world of money, and there is the world of your passion. The trick is to find where the two intersect."

Doing what you love, what excites you, thrills you and delights you, puts you in touch with your spiritual path. Doing what makes money, what takes care of you and your loved ones, puts you on the path of being a mystic in the marketplace.

INNER FULFILLMENT BRINGS CASH

"I don't want money," a friend told me. "I want inner fulfillment."

He originally told me he wanted to make $600,000 this year. I went to the trouble of giving him a personalized strategy to create the wealth. Now he says he doesn't want cash, he wants inner satisfaction. At first I thought he was expressing a fear about money. Not now.

"If you shoot for inner fulfillment through total services to others," I told him, "and if you remember to charge for what you do, then you'll get the cash you want. The money comes as a by-product of serving yourself and others in a way that obeys business laws."

There are a lot of books out on how to manipulate people. What they overlook is the long-term effect you have.

You can persuade someone to buy your service, but if they regret their decision, or if you don't serve them in the way you promised, what will they say about you?

Michael LeBeowolf, in his outstanding book, *Keep Customers For Life* said your unhappy customers will tell from 6 to 9 people about your lousy service. That's a lot of negative PR.

"Focus on serving people," I told my friend, "and be sure to charge a healthy fee. People will accept the bill if you take care of them. You'll feel fulfilled and so will they."

It's just as much a mistake to focus ONLY on making money as it is to focus ONLY on inner fulfillment. The real fulfillment comes from a balance of the two.

Hugh Prather once said that too many people waste energy trying to materialize the things they want through affirmations, visualization, rituals and so forth. He suggested you simply take a job you like. Working on the mental plane isn't enough. You can do all the inner work you like, but at some point you have to walk out into the business arena and actually DO something of value to others.

TAKE THE HINT

"The universe sent me a clear message not to do that" is a line I hear almost daily. Here's an example:

"I tried to get a teaching job at the college but more than 200 people applied and I was passed up," a dear friend told me. He's got three degrees, more workshop experience than anyone I know, natural skills as a therapist, and yet he's working for minimum wage as a salesman, at a job he hates!

"I guess the universe is telling me to forget teaching," he shrugged.

"How do you know you aren't supposed to try harder?" I asked. "Persistence is more important than talent or luck, you know. Calvin Coolidge said so himself."

"I've been trying for four years now. I can take a hint."

"How many applications did you fill out in four years?"

"I dunno. Probably 25 or 30. A lot."

"You've barely begun the process," I said. "Look, Colonel Sanders was an old man knocking door-to-door trying to sell his chicken recipe, and he got rejection after rejection. If you were he, would you give up after 25 rejections?"

"Maybe."

"Would you stop trying after 100 rejections?"

"It'd be a clear sign the universe didn't want me to go that way. I'd stop trying, for sure."

"Listen to this, my friend. Colonel Sanders got more than one THOUSAND rejections before he made his first sale!"

"He did?"

"Do you want to be a teacher?" I asked my friend.

"Yea."

"Then why stop now? Twenty-five noes is nothing."

"The universe doesn't seem to want me to do that," he said.

"I think you're blaming the universe," I declared. "Take responsibility for what you are doing. Reading 25 noes as a sign to stop trying is YOUR interpretation. It has nothing to do with the universe."

"I don't know," my friend stammered. "I need a sign to tell me I'm on the right track."

"Maybe this whole conversation is a sign to keep moving forward toward your dream," I persisted. "Just what do you think the universe is, anyway?"

"It's everything. Life itself."

"YOU are the universe," I declared. "People keep saying they can do miracles, but then they don't do them. They keep throwing away their responsibility on some 'universe' somewhere. It's just a sneaky way to refer to a belief in God or some sort of supreme being."

"How am I supposed to know what to do next?"

"Be honest with yourself. Under your fears and concerns is a knowing about what to do. If you weren't afraid, what would you do?"

"Teach."

"Go for it then," I said.

Like my friend, too many New Age-oriented people try to read events as messages from "the universe." If you know what you want and move toward it, everything that happens will just be part of the road. Even a rejection or block could be seen as a challenge for you to think more creatively or resolve your will.

BUSINESS PRINCIPLES

Here are a few thoughts to consider:

If you don't do what you love, you will lose business. People will notice your lack of enthusiasm and enjoyment. This teaches you to follow your bliss.

If you don't listen to your clients or to your supervisor, you won't stay in business. People want to be served. They want what they say they want, and they want it when they say they want it. This teaches you to serve.

If you don't do what others ask of you, or pay you to do, you will lose business. The people you deal with in business usually hire you to satisfy a specific need. You have to concentrate on THEM, not yourself, in order to stay in business. This teaches you to let go of your ego.

If you don't do your work with skill and precision, you will lose business. In today's world there is a lot of competition for similar skills and services. The trick is to be a professional at what you do. This teaches you mastery.

If you don't sell what you do, people will not buy it. Everything you say and do delivers a message about you and your work. If you don't realize that you are a salesperson, you will not stay in business. This teaches you communication.

THE MAN NOBODY KNOWS

Back in the mid-1920s Bruce Barton wrote a best-selling book called *The Man Nobody Knows*. In it Barton described Jesus as not only a great spiritual leader, but an effective business manager as well. After all, Barton pointed out, Jesus spent more time in the marketplace than the synagogue.

Think about it.

AFTERWORD

The chapters you just read all took place more than twenty years ago.

What happened after those experiences?

I continued to struggle, to grow, to move towards my dreams and goals---but with only baby steps. The experiences I had all helped me grow, mature, and evolve. But it wasn't until I discovered the work of Jerry and Esther Hicks that things began to really cook.

Jerry and Esther are friends as well as clients of mine. I've now known them well over 12 years. I wrote the foreword to one of their books. I've written a few of their national magazine ads. Today they are becoming famous for their feel-good messages.

They distribute the message of going for your dreams by following what feels best in any moment. Through them I learned of the power of intention, emotion and letting go. You can learn more about them at **http://www.abraham-hicks.com**.

But I also found their message lacking. It didn't always work for me, or for many of the people I knew. I discovered that if you carried a belief in you that was counter to your intention, that belief could sabotage your success, no matter how good you felt. In short, there had to be a way to get clear of those limiting beliefs.

That's where my discovery of Jonathan, the healer I wrote about in my book *Spiritual Marketing*, made such a dramatic difference in my life. Once I began to work with him, and to look at and release my limiting beliefs, my life began to soar. Books began to get published. I moved into a nice, safe house in a better part of town. Intentions about my finances, happiness, and health all began to manifest. I even became a celebrity online, and am now considered an Internet marketing pioneer.

And as a result of my work with Jonathan, combined with my experiences studying and knowing Jerry and Esther Hicks, I developed my own five-step formula for achieving your dreams. I explained it all in my book *Spiritual Marketing*. If you want to know the rest of my story, read that book.

Also, if you are wondering what healers and helpers I work with these days, there are several:

Ann Taylor Harcus at **http://www.innerhealing.com**
e-mail: miracles22@aol.com

Dr. Roopa Chari at **http://www.charicenter.com**
e-mail: ChariCenter@aol.com

Mandy Evans at **http://www.mandyevans.com**
e-mail: Mandy@MandyEvans.com

Art Martin e-mail: artmartin@mindspring.com

John Harricharan at **http://www.insight2000.com**
e-mail: jhh711@insight2000.com

Meanwhile, thank you for reading this book. I trust you enjoyed it, were inspired, and maybe even experienced insights that will help you, too, go for and achieve your dreams.

I wonder what you will do next.

Dare something worthy.

ABOUT THE AUTHOR

Dr. Joe Vitale is the author of the international #1 bestseller *Spiritual Marketing,* the #1 bestselling e-book *Hypnotic Writing,* the #1 bestselling Nightingale-Conant audioprogram *The Power of Outrageous Marketing,* and numerous other works, including the global bestseller *The Greatest Money-Making Secret in History!*

His most recent book, co-authored with Jo Han Mok, is *The E-Code: 47 Secrets for Making Money Online Almost Instantly.* He is currently writing a book with Dr. Robert Anthony called *Spiritual Marketing in Action!*

Joe is also an ordained minister, a certified metaphysical practitioner, a certified hypnotherapist, and a certified Chi Kung healer. He also holds a doctoral degree in Metaphysical Science.

Dr. Vitale currently lives in the Hill Country outside of Austin, Texas, with his pets and his love, Nerissa.

For a catalog of his books and tapes, to read dozens of free articles by him, or to sign up for his popular free e-newsletter, see his main website at **http://www.mrfire.com** or visit his new website at **http://www.DrJoeVitale.com**.

For more copies of this book, or for copies of *Spiritual Marketing* or *The Greatest Money-Making Secret in History!,* by Joe Vitale, please visit www.amazon.com or www.1stbooks.com or call 1-888-280-7715

Printed in the United States
60467LVS00010B/76-123

9 781410 774606